MERCY
WINS

LEARNING MERCY IN
A MERCILESS AGE

Dale Anderson

OASIS HOUSE – KANSAS CITY, MISSOURI

Dedication

*To Cheryl, Jordan and Bethany—you have
taught me much about mercy.
I love you!*

Contents

Foreword

Mercy is the universal necessity—we all need it desperately and owe it to our fellow mankind. No topic addresses the crux of the broken human condition more directly than mercy.

Dale Anderson devotes the second chapter of this book to the context in which the word *mercy* occurs in the Bible for the first time. God extended mercy to Lot by pulling him out of Sodom by the hand, even as he hesitated to leave. From that story I have come to define mercy as the kindness of God to get you where you need to go, in spite of yourself.

Really, that's what mercy is all about. It's about helping someone, in his weakness and dysfunction and sin, get pointed in the right direction—even when he himself tends to veer off course.

When God appeared to Moses on the mountain in a visible manifestation, and then spoke His name to Moses, the first thing out of His mouth was not, "I am holy." Rather, the first attribute He revealed about Himself was this: "'The LORD God, merciful'" (Exod. 34:6). That means that God is merciful at the very foundations of His being. It's usually His first response to us—over and over and over again.

With this book in hand, bask in the extravagant mercies of your God who loves you. Then, when you set the book down, be merciful to others.

That's what the Christian life is all about: receiving mercy and then giving it to others. It's much easier to give it once you've received it. You are merciful to someone else when you labor to help them get pointed toward their upward calling in Christ. You can't get someone else into her destiny, but you can help her to get moving in the right direction.

When you do, you come under one of the most potent promises that came from Jesus' lips: "'Blessed are the merciful, for they shall obtain mercy'" (Matt. 5:7).

That's why you're gripping this book. You're here until mercy permeates every fiber of your being.

Thank you, Dale, for giving us such a candid, heartfelt, personal window into your own journey. As a result, your words empower us to become ignited with the wonder and reality of God's mercy. But we're not stopping there, Dale. We're going to take your baton and run with it, that the mercies of God might extend through us to a world that so desperately needs it.

Bob Sorge
Kansas City, Missouri
June 2010

CHAPTER 1

The Call to Mercy

*"He has shown you, O man, what is good; and what
does the* Lord *require of you but to do justly,* to love
mercy, *and to walk humbly with your God?"*
(Mic. 6:8, emphasis added).

I've always been captivated by pleasure and power. If I
can experience both at the same time, in the same event,
I'm really revved! In June 2007, I had the most powerful *and*
pleasurable encounter with the Lord I've ever had in my life
since my conversion. In fact, this moment was so powerful it
changed my life forever.

I was in a season of consecration, setting my heart before
the Lord. I did something I had never done before—a three-
day silent fast. With each passing hour of the fast, my heart
was softening in response to my sensing the nearness of Holy
Spirit. Then one Sunday after the fast, I went into my little
sanctuary, my office at home, in response to the prompting of
Holy Spirit to set aside the afternoon for seclusion and prayer.
It's my secret place, small and intimate. I feel the Lord there.
It's where I can shut the door and spend time alone with Jesus (Matt. 6:7). So after clearing my desk and sending some
e-mails that Sunday, I sat back in my chair and said, "Here I
am."

What happened next still moves me. A phrase of Scripture immediately invaded my mind and came off my lips, "James, the Lord's brother." It's a phrase used by Paul in Galatians 1:19. No sooner did those words come out of my mouth than a real tangible presence entered into my office.

All I can tell you is someone from heaven visited me that afternoon. I believe it was the Lord, and I was overcome by His presence. My first impulse was to get low and kiss the ground. I remember sobbing so intensely that I was physically impacted. I mean, my heart was pounding, and I was having a very difficult time catching my breath. And just as I gained control of myself and settled my heart and hyperventilating lungs, I found myself saying the phrase again, "James, the Lord's brother."

With each repetition of the phrase, I felt as if a hand pressed a page of paper to my chest, and the page seemed to dissolve right into it. That process repeated itself for much of the afternoon until finally, emotionally spent and physically exhausted, it suddenly stopped as quickly as it had started.

Just as the presence of the Lord began to lift, my heart reverberated with His parting words, "I want you to teach the letter of James at the Bible school. I want this to be a book, yes books. This is My mercy to you. Will you do it?" Then as now, at the time of my writing this book, I was teaching at the Forerunner School of Ministry at the International House of Prayer in Kansas City (IHOP-KC).

Let me clarify something else at this point. You see, I wasn't even studying the book of James when all this occurred. I was meditating on other books in my prayer life then. Have you ever read James? Do you know what's in that book? If you want me to be honest, James was one of those books I generally ignored, you know, accidentally on purpose!

I do remember, however, what I was seeking the Lord for during that season. I was asking the Lord to teach me about mercy and true justice, to remove human sentiment and unbelief from my life. I was asking Him to deal with a deeply rooted religious spirit I felt existed in my heart. I was asking Him to release true faith and to fill me with His wisdom. What I didn't realize was all that I was asking for is contained in James's letter.

What I didn't understand that day was God *was* answering my request, writing His Word on my heart and setting it deep in my spirit. He was downloading, as it were, the content from James's letter and the full emotion of His heart from that book.

Beloved, there was a cry in my heart in that hour to know the truth about mercy and justice. I wanted to know what *God* thought about mercy, what *He* thought about justice. I wanted to know how the cross could be the pinnacle of God's mercy, grace and justice all in the same moment when the worst of mankind was revealed. I wanted to know how Jesus' mercy could so move the human heart, bringing real and lasting change. I wanted to understand what it was to be deeply connected to Father God's love forever. I had so many unanswered questions inside, and I was desperate for the answers. I wanted to touch the uninsulated electrical current of God. I wanted change. I was hungry for more of Him and wanted to be filled (Matt. 5:6).

The day the Lord touched me with the book of James, I was asked a question. He asked me if I would teach and write about it. I said *yes* and haven't looked back. I've had several hard lessons since that day. I've been learning mercy and justice in daily life. I've met them in Jesus just as I believe James did. In fact, I believe mercy was where James met Jesus, his half-brother, at the deepest level. I also believe that, as James touched the mercy of Jesus, he was transformed instantaneously.

How do I know this? In part, I've experienced such transformation in my own life and also witnessed it in the lives of others. But we see specifically in the book of James the writer's own revelation when he says, "For judgment is without mercy to the one who has shown no mercy. *Mercy triumphs over judgment*" (James 2:13, emphasis added).

Friends, all my life I've been hungry for the power of God's mercy. Since my conversion, I've been a student of His emotions, and I've been asking much about mercy. I want to know what kind of power is resident in mercy that when released by the heart of God into the lives of men great change transpires. I've always wanted to know, how does mercy win over judgment? (James 2:13) How can mercy and judgment manifest in the same event in one moment of time?

But more importantly, I've wanted to know intimately the mind and heart that conceived mercy, especially as it's expressed in the cross. What kind of mind thinks of such things? You see, I think the true power of mercy is found in the Person who originated it. The gift of mercy is great, but I want to know the Creator of mercy. To know mercy and justice, we must find the Person who created them in the first place. Otherwise, we come away with only powerless concepts; we end up without the very power we need to employ those concepts in our daily lives.

In June of 2007, I had a revelation of something the Lord has been teaching me daily for many years. I began a pilgrimage to the heart of God, a search for true mercy and justice. I accepted an assignment that will likely consume the rest of my days and be one of my primary preoccupations in life.

I am on a search. I've had a few lessons along the road to doing justly and loving mercy. But one thing I am still longing for is certain: *I desire the power to walk out true justice and real mercy.* I want the reality of this power in my life that it might touch down with sincerity in my daily context.

I want to touch the pleasure *and* power of God's mercy, and I believe you do, too. We all need to touch the mercy of Jesus. We all need to find the grip of His grace as He embraces and holds our hearts in His love. We all need to discover the truth of His ways that go much deeper than the half-truths and short-baked realities of life. Every day we are offered false glory, seductive to the eyes but bitter and unsatisfying to the soul. We need to touch true mercy. We need new definitions of His grace so that we are not fooled by human sentiment or smooth-talking charlatans.

We are moving into a new season in the history of humanity, and it appears that apocalypse is in the air. The clouds of nature are boiling, nations are rattling their sabers, finances are failing, marriages are miscarrying, presidents are promiscuous, and believers are unbelieving. All of these are merely the signs of man's broken choices. These are the signs of humanity's boredom with life as it knows it and of its constant search for the next greatest fix of pleasure or power.

What we really need is the power of His mercy to redefine us, to redefine our thinking. It's not enough to know true mercy; we want to be change agents of mercy. We want to cover the earth with the glory of His mercy as the waters cover the sea. We want his mercy to triumph, we want mercy to win.

The journey starts with one small step for man, and one giant leap for God.

I find many reasons to reach for this, but one outshines the rest. I want my life built on foundations that can never be shaken or destroyed. His mercy is one stone in the whole foundation.

Yes, storms are coming, not just natural ones like hurricanes and tornadoes, but those that would cause man's heart to melt with fear. In those moments, false foundations are like castles of sand touched by the waves of life; they melt into the surf with no evidence of prior existence.

I don't want that to be my or my children's story. I don't want that to be your story either. I want to stand strong in moments of shaking. I want to stand firm on the foundation of Jesus' love and mercy, giving direction like a lighthouse to those who built on foolish foundations. I want to stand strong and give an eternal perspective with merciful options to those melting in the heat. And I want my children to do the same. This is what I want, and it's what I hope you want as well.

Friends, I invite you to journey with me through the pages of this book. Let Holy Spirit take you by the hand and introduce you to the power of victorious mercy inherent in the Trinity. From the cross of Jesus Christ to the throne of Father, mercy is the fragrance and healing balm of the God-head. And you and I are called to learn and do mercy. Our lives are to be a living definition of the mercy of Jesus. His Spirit, the Spirit of Truth, will guide and empower you to learn and to show mercy in this merciless age.

CHAPTER 2

Mercy Defined

*"And while he lingered, the men took hold of his hand...
the LORD being merciful to him..." (Gen. 19:16).*

There is a law in biblical scholarship called the *law of first mention*. It teaches us that we find definitions for biblical terms, attributes of God and so on as we study their first occurrence in the Scriptures. Using that law and applying it to *mercy* or *merciful*, we find ourselves in Genesis 19 with the story of Lot and the destruction of Sodom and Gomorrah.

I have to tell you that this shocked me. I was thinking our first example might be found in the story of Elijah and the widow's son, the one whom Elijah raised from the dead. I thought it would be a story full of love and grace (which this is) but devoid of deep sinful patterns or heated judgment. The story of Lot and Sodom, the city in which he lived, has it all. It definitely tells us much about God's mercy, but it's His mercy within the context of sinners and judgment. Because of this context, the story of Lot and Sodom more clearly shows us what mercy is and what it's not!

Whether God showed mercy to Lot because of His love for him or in answer to Abraham's intercession (Gen. 18) isn't fully clear. I have a feeling it was a little of both.

We learn in the passage how Sodom was a city with ho-
mosexuals as found by the Angel of the Lord who spoke to
Abraham. The story opens with Lot seated at the city gate
watching. What he was watching for we don't know, but it
was clear he was there. Back in Lot's day, the city elders sat
daily at the city gate to oversee business transactions, take
counsel and watch over the comings and goings of the people
in and out of the city. On this occasion, Lot appeared to be
alone at the gate. We are told that all the men of the city
later came to Lot's house and asked for the two angels. My
thinking is that Lot was one of the few men, maybe even the
only man, of the city not given to homosexuality. Although
his two sons-in-law obviously were married to his daughters,
I'm not sure about them in regard to this subject. All we have
in the text is they didn't want to leave Sodom in the end.

When the angels first came to the city, Lot recognized
them and immediately brought them into his home. He
showed by the urgency of his hospitality that he knew what
would happen next. He knew his city! From this point on in
the story, everything went downhill.

The men of the city came to Lot's house, looking for the
two newcomers and wanting to have sex with them. They
asked, "Where are the men who came to you tonight? Bring
them out to us that we may know them carnally!" (Gen.
19:5).

This city was completely given over to the gay agenda
of its day. The men were charging after strange flesh, deeply
marked by wickedness as they pursued false pictures of God
and false idols. They had rejected the ways of God and His
design for sexual intimacy—namely, one man for one woman within the love bonds of a marriage covenant!

Then there was Lot; he was oppressed by such con-
duct day in and day out. He was a watchman of righteousness who was accused of being judgmental for calling such

behavior *wicked*. How does one stand for righteousness in the midst of wickedness and not be touched, dirtied or soiled in some way by such filthy acts?

Under the wicked smog of Sodom's atmosphere, Lot offered his two single daughters. In protecting the two angels, he was willing for his daughters to be raped rather than hand these heaven-sent messengers over to the lewdness and perversion of his city. Though he was not participating in its sexual sin, his mind was being affected by the licentious atmosphere of the city. A fog of oppression was clouding Lot's thought life. His sons-in-law did not take him seriously, and he, his wife and daughters were slow to respond to the command of the Angel of the Lord to flee for high ground.

Is any of this starting to sound familiar? Hesitation, debating God's plan, our minds cloudy and dull?!

But God who is tender and merciful, not willing that any should perish and not willing to sweep the righteous away with the wicked, saved Lot's life. The merciful act, the thing that reveals the mercy of God to us in this chapter, is found in verse 16 with these simple words, "And while *he lingered,* the men *took hold of his hand,* his wife's hand, and the hands of his two daughters, the LORD *being merciful to him,* and *they brought him out,* and *set him outside the city*" (emphasis added).

Do you see this? Lot was still debating with the Angel whether to leave or not! The demonically supercharged atmosphere of the city was so oppressive that his mind was getting confused and contaminated. He needed help and fast! He needed mercy because he hesitated.

Not only that, but when the Angel got him outside the city, Lot still debated on where he wanted to go. The Angel said, "Escape to the mountains, lest you be destroyed" (Gen. 19:17). He was directing Lot to go toward Abraham's territory, and Lot said, "Let me go to Zoar," which was another city in the valley (v. 22).

Do you see Lot's lingering hesitation? He was still tormented in his mind about what he should do—wanting to love the lost but tormented by their lifestyles.

The Angel of the Lord delivered Lot and his family. Literally, God delivered Lot. God took him by the hand and walked him outside the city and told him to run.

Reflect on this for a moment. The first time the word *merciful* is used in the Bible is when God takes a man out of a wicked city about to collide with His wrath and when the man knowing that judgment day had come still hesitates! If that's not mercy, I don't know what is.

Think right now of the times the Lord has taken you by the hand and walked you out of situations where judgment was looming and where you were still trying to negotiate with Him.

We have this thought, and I don't really know where it came from, but it is an unstated rule that isn't of the Lord. This rule tells us that we have to deserve mercy before we get mercy. Can I just be clear with you here? If that were the case, none of us would be here.

Mercy is at the very core of who God is. It is Love's twin that motivates the heart of God. He acts toward us in mercy not because we deserve it, but because it's His nature to act in such a way.

This is also why Jesus exhorts us to learn mercy. In essence, He's telling us that it's not at the core of who we are, but when we say *yes* to God, He starts revealing to us who He is and how we should live. If God's Son is merciful, then His Son's wife—His wife—should also be. At this moment, she's not that merciful, but she will be before He returns.

Lot hesitated. He lingered. The literal meaning of the word was *delayed in the face of the impending judgments of God*. God pitied Lot, despite the hesitation, for God knew his heart.

We can see Lot's hesitation and delay, but can we see

the mercy and compassion of the Lord for His friend Lot? We see Lot as dirty and not completely without guilt. Yet the Lord saw him as righteous in Sodom, though tormented and oppressed. It was time to remove Lot from his torment and oppression. It was time to give him a fresh start.

The Lord knows our hearts. He heard the cry of Lot's heart, knowing that as He responded Lot would still struggle.

Consider something with me. In Genesis 18 when the Angel of the Lord tells Abraham that the outcry against Sodom was very great (v. 20), who was crying out? We see when the Angel visited the city that all the men, save Lot and his sons-in-law, wanted to assault the visitors. But at the time of their leaving, Lot's sons-in-law didn't listen to him. His wife turned back, longing for the life she had in Sodom. The daughters were upset they had to move and lose their husbands. So who was crying out? Lot! I think it was Lot.

As we sit stuck in our ruts of past failure, wishing we hadn't failed but still chained by it, there is a groan inside us that only God can hear. He is coming. He will take us by the hand. He will help us.

Come, let's return to the Lord. His judgments and disciplines may sting for the moment, but in the magnitude of His mercy, we will find safe ground and a new place to live.

CHAPTER 3

Tender Mercies

*"The Lord is gracious and full of compassion, slow
to anger and great in mercy. The Lord is good to all, and His
tender mercies are over all His works" (Ps. 145:8–9).*

God is tender and affectionate. His tenderness is expressed powerfully in His mercy toward us.

Mercy is God's gift to us, erupting from the depths of His compassionate nature. He looked down at our lowly estate, and unlike all the other gods of the earth who remain in the heavens distant and disconnected, our God came down to us. He stooped down and filled our emptiness. He sought connection with us. He became one of us, died like a criminal. He did all of this to fulfill a plan in Father's heart that would rub healing balm into the open wounds, into the mighty carved canyons, separating us from Him.

I've discovered His mercy often comes cloaked in humanity. My own flesh and blood—my wife Cheryl, son Jordan and daughter Beth—are three such mercy gifts, wrapped in all their human frailty and divine grace.

Ours is a typical family with all the laughter and tears, the beauty and blemishes of real people. We face the temptations and challenges common to all. We're just an ordinary family in love with an extraordinary God.

Recently, we celebrated Beth's eighteenth birthday. Oh, what a story of God's tender mercy!

We adopted Beth eighteen years ago from a small town hospital in Romania. She was petite, very sick, quite thin and all alone. She had been conceived in rape and born to a very young mother who, while pregnant with Beth, was sent for an abortion three times. Thankfully, she never went through with one. Clearly, the Lord's hand was on Beth from her mother's womb.

On the evening of Beth's eighteenth birthday, we called her out and as a family commissioned her to walk with God all her days and to contend for the faith. Scenes from our lives together played on the screens of our minds that night. We remembered and recounted so many shared experiences. With her loved ones around her, we laid hands on her and spoke prophetically into her life. We reminded her where she had come from and heartily agreed with the desires of her heart to cook for little kids in an orphanage somewhere on the earth.

More specifically, I recalled when Cheryl brought Beth home to me. Beth was so cute, vulnerable, fragile and cold. By cold, I mean she appeared emotionally shut down. And as we got better acquainted with her, we became very familiar with the emotional baggage that weighed on her little psyche.

Each day we saw she didn't want affection. She didn't like it when I held her to feed her. She was cranky when others tried to interact and connect with her. She wasn't positively responsive to our attempts to love on her. She would smile, not when we attempted to coo and cuddle with her— no, she smiled when untouched and left alone. Beth made it very clear to us early on that no one was going to love her and that she would do her best to reject any form of affection offered her.

One story in particular demonstrates perfectly what we all confronted when trying to develop our relationships with

Beth. I can smile now about it, but it wasn't very comical at the time.

I remember every morning, when the kids were little, Beth would wake up, run to her older brother who stood with arms open to her and sock him in the stomach. Every day she would punch him, and every day he would still stand there waiting to hug her. I often thought, *Jordan, watch out! She's going to hit you!* And she would. I think the Lord just gave him grace!

Meanwhile, Cheryl and I prayed about this and Beth's other behaviors. Although she had come to us so seemingly broken, she became a physically and emotionally strong child. This led us into a season where we prayed a lot for her, asking God to identify and break the strongholds over her life.

One day, while Cheryl was walking in the park near our apartment, she heard Holy Spirit say that Beth had a spirit of rejection and that she was battling an orphan spirit. We took those words to prayer, and the very next day the Lord confirmed them in a pamphlet written by John and Paula Sanford. To this day, we don't know who mailed it to us. Arriving the next day via regular post, with no return address, the pamphlet was about parents praying for the life of their adopted child. We rejoiced! God caused our faith to awaken to see that something actually could change for Beth.

After reading the pamphlet, we started to employ the principles suggested in it. We asked Holy Spirit for specific Scripture verses to pray over her as she slept. We learned that, while the body and conscience may be sleeping, the spirit is still open and awake.

We started to pray Psalm 139 over Beth, using very specific Scriptures highlighted to us by the Lord. We learned the value of reading Scriptures as prayer over each other and our family. As Beth's father, I spoke, more like whispered, phrases from the tender verses, phrases that were expressions of my heart for her as a father. In a spiritual way that night, I went to war against the dark influence telling her soul she was alone (vv. 7–10) and did not belong in our home.

The very next day the warfare intensified. Beth woke up with sores all over her face. They appeared open and cracked, some of them oozing with pus. It was horrible, but we soldiered on. We kept laying hands on her and whispering our statements of love over her. Each night we would contend for her as she slept. We would pray and gently rub ointment into her sores, touching her so as not to wake her. Night after night I'd reach over her crib to pray for her, placing my hand on her arm or lightly touching her back. No one knew what was going on with her face. The doctors couldn't explain the breakout, but I knew what it was. It was a negative spiritual reaction to my desire to claim her as my daughter. Whatever oppressive spirit it was, the bonding process with her was failing. One night, two nights, three nights...nothing, or so we thought.

Then the Lord added to the plan. Before putting her in bed, I was impressed by Him to hold her on my chest and not let her go no matter what, and I determined to do so.

Our bedtime routine became an all-out war fought on many battlefronts. Beth knew it was coming and really didn't like it. I held her to my chest, and she twisted and turned, kicked and elbowed, bit and head-butted. I thought I was in a professional wrestling cage match! One night, two nights, three nights...nothing.

Then the break came. We were in one of our evening wrestling matches. She bit and kicked me and started to twist and turn. She turned over onto her back so I couldn't see her face. Within five minutes of this particularly hard bout, I heard her sigh, not quietly or quickly. She sighed deeply as if she were releasing all the air out of her body. She stopped moving and rested there on my chest.

If my heart could leap, it leapt that night. For the first

time, I thought she had fallen asleep in my arms—my little girl asleep in *my* embrace. Once I believed she was sound asleep, I started to slide off the bed in order to get up and place her in her crib. Suddenly, she cranked her neck around and looked straight into my eyes. What I saw in those eyes at that moment was absolutely stunning. I saw in the Spirit that I had an open opportunity to speak into her heart while she was awake. I felt that my words would affect her significantly. I knew I was writing my initials in the wet cement of her life, leaving my whole palm print, as it were, behind with my name on it.

I called her by her first name, "Bethany," I said. "I'm your daddy. I love you, and Jesus loves you, and we'll never let you go." She smiled at me and turned over, placing her ear on my chest. And then she fell asleep.

As we prayed over her that night, we anointed her face with cream. She was still suffering from the sores on her face. As we finished one side of her face, she turned her head, though still asleep, to expose her other cheek. We spread the cream on that side as well and went to bed. We sensed something significant had happened.

In my bed, I cried myself to sleep for I heard the whisper of Father in my own spirit, *You know, Dale, you're just like Beth. You kick and squirm, bite and elbow but won't settle into My love for you. When will I hear the sigh of surrender from you?*

For the first time in my life, Holy Spirit let me feel the deep loneliness, rejection and pain in my own heart. I got in touch with my own fight to be loved that night. I was doing all the right religious things a Christian man should do while trying to stay away from the things I shouldn't do and failing at both. All my inner brokenness was manifesting outwardly like the sores on my daughter's face.

Anger erupted daily at my inability to love my life the way I could, and therefore love others well. Looking in the mirror every day, I loathed the man I saw. I numbed the pain in late night TV which is never healthy.

In all this, I thought my perceptions of myself were actually God's thoughts about me. I was shouting at myself, pointing continually at the darkness of my heart. I was full of rejection just like my daughter. My relationship with my wife was distant and cold, not knowing the true meaning of intimacy. Yes, in one night I touched it all and was overwhelmed.

Then the very verses I was so powerfully using to set my daughter free began whispering to my own soul. The tender mercy Jesus had given me to pour on my daughter was washing over me. As I pondered the embrace of Father, I settled just a little bit more into His chest. The war wasn't over that night for me, but a significant journey had begun. I realized that God had given us grace to choose Beth for us and, in a way, us for Beth. We were both applying the healing ointment to one another—the ointment of God's tender mercies—that we might see we are never cast off or forgotten but are continually loved and always welcomed home.

The way He had shown me to contend for Beth's freedom had broken the hard shell of my own heart, making me realize He was winning my love, bonding to me in the same way I was reaching for my daughter. Though there would be many battles to wage after that for both Beth and me, something significant came to us. We received a revelation of His tender mercy, a revelation of His unending love.

The next morning, Beth woke up and ran to her brother who stood with his arms open to her. This time something was different. I didn't see her fist clenched. I didn't see her punch her brother's stomach as I had so many other mornings. For the first time in her life, at almost two years of age, Beth offered her first hug. Wrapping her arms around her brother, she squeezed him. He grabbed her and smiled.

I believe it was God's justice that Jordan was the first

family member to get the first hug from Beth. So many mornings he opened his arms to her, and so many mornings he was met with a solid hard punch. He never hit back and was always faithful to offer her open arms no matter what she had done to him the previous morning. He was manifesting mercy every day, and then as his sister's life was changing, he was still offering mercy.

I finish this chapter with the question the Lord gave me. *When will He hear the sigh of surrender from you?*

I learned a powerful lesson from my two children. Jordan evidenced for me the new mercy Father shows me each and every morning. Beth showed me how to hug His mercy. In His faithfulness, I know He will never let me go. He stands facing you and me with open arms. Will we rush to Him with a fist to fight and a mind to wrestle? Or will we release the sigh of surrender—will we capitulate?

He's waiting! Let's run to Him and embrace His tender mercy!

CHAPTER 4

The Internship of Mercy

"'Now go and learn the meaning of this Scripture: "I want
you to be merciful; I don't want your sacrifices"'"
(Matt. 9:13, NLT).

As the last chapter illustrated, showing and embracing mercy are taught. My children's own interactions instructed me how to give and receive mercy. And they learned how to *do* mercy as they exercised it in their daily living. *How to do mercy* sounds odd, I know, but it is what we learn as followers of Christ.

I have a strong conviction that we learn mercy through the ups and downs, the highs and lows—the ordinary stuff we call *life*. As we deal with the daily events of our lives, Holy Spirit teaches and trains us in mercy. He educates us how to do it—how to accept mercy and how to be merciful ourselves.

In this chapter's opening verse, Jesus tells the Pharisees (and His disciples, and us vicariously) to "go and learn" the meaning of Hosea 6:6 ("I desire mercy"). He wants them to discover what He means when He says He wants *them* to be merciful. How would they go and learn that God wanted them to be merciful without also learning *how* to be merciful?

Jesus' plan was to school them—if they would be schooled,

that is. And He wants us to learn to be merciful too. I believe
He has a special training program for teaching us to do mercy. I like to compare it to an internship. It's the kind of school
that uses the "hands-on" approach. Yes, it means homework,
tests and learning in the context of community with other
learners. It means trial and error, success and failure, walking, running, stumbling and falling and, most importantly,
getting back up and trying once more. The internship of
mercy has teachers anointed and gifted to impart and guide.
These help us to learn mercy as we give it or ask for it.

In God's school, there are times when we don't ask for
mercy, but because of who God is and the desires burning
within Him, He gives it. He gives it even when we don't ask
for or deserve it. He gives it because of who He is, this Man
of mercy. He gives it because someone may ask on our behalf
as Abraham interceded for Lot. He gives it because, when
mercy is felt and experienced, it grips the human heart forever and calls for a gratitude that changes the way we live.

Matthew 12:7 reads similarly to Matthew 9:13. It says,
"'But if you had known what this means, "I desire mercy and
not sacrifice," you would not have condemned the guiltless.'"

We need to understand the meaning of *known* as it is
used in this verse. It is more than informational and cogni-
tive in nature. It actually refers to experiential understanding. Once we've experienced God's desire for mercy—once
we've learned it and known it—we won't condemn those
who are innocent or guiltless.

That's simple enough, isn't it? But let's keep looking.
Digging deeper, I'm struck by the converse of the last three
words. If we changed the last three words to read opposite of
what they do now, the ending of the verse would read as follows: "You would not have *acquitted the guilty*."

Acquitting the guilty does a couple of things. First, it enables the guilty to continue practicing the negative behavior
that endangers the greater community and ultimately ruins

it. Second, mercy is done violence. How so? The fear of the Lord is robbed from the guilty. When the guilty do not fear discipline, punishment or judgment, their hearts grow strong and bold in the sinful behavior they perpetuate.

Judgment is one form of God's mercy. If the guilty have to do jail time, it can be viewed as an act of mercy! Serving time in prison or facing penalties for wrongdoing provides the guilty the opportunity to face what they've done and reflect on it. Potentially, they can contemplate about what they must do to be restored to the community. Judgment grants the guilty a chance to change their behavior—to repent and be changed. I also believe judgment provides mercy to those innocents who no longer are subjected to the behaviors of the guilty. We don't like to speak often of mercy in this way and give it this definition. But I believe it is a part of how we learn mercy.

Let's move on to another thought about learning to do mercy.

We see in Scripture that Jesus learned mercy. He told us that no servant is greater than his master (John 13:16). That statement tells me He never expects us to go somewhere or do something that He hasn't gone or done first. If I couple that with His call for us to go and learn mercy, then it stands to reason that He learned it somewhere Himself.

To be the human sacrifice on the cross for you and me, He had to walk our road so that the sacrifice would be fully just. I believe, as a human, Jesus cultivated mercy. And I believe He learned it from two sources: His earthly family in His earthly home and His heavenly Father.

Being taught by His Father in heaven is easier for us to believe. We all think Jesus came with some implanted computer chip already programmed to speak, act and live perfectly! Like Father, like son, right? Have you ever considered Jesus' training period before His baptism by John in the Jordan River and the subsequent onset of His earthly ministry?

I think Jesus had a thirty-year internship hidden in the hills of Nazareth, working in Joseph's carpenter shop. How long would it take you and me to develop a nature and character that would say and speak only what heavenly Father told us to say (John 12:49)?

Let me ask you another question? Did your son come hardwired with a fully operational and mature "mercy software program"? Don't say *yes* because I won't believe you. I think you had to train him in it.

This may be uncomfortable for us to consider. After all, Jesus is God. He's the King of kings. He knows and sees all, and He's perfect in every way. He's fully God yet still fully Man! He's in His resurrected body (and that's *some* body!), but there is a Man in heaven at the right hand of Father. He is God the Son, second person of the Trinity, and He's a *Man* (1 Tim. 2:5)!

I believe Father helped His Son cultivate the learning or experiencing of mercy through the earthly family He placed Him in. It's the front line, primary source of learning we all first experience. Our earthly families affect so much of our thinking and behavior in life. It is our first school!

This first school teaches us to talk, eat, dress ourselves, tie our shoes, write our names, love and play—the list is endless. We receive most of this education before we start first grade!

Can you imagine Jesus' home as He grew up in Nazareth? We probably don't ever think about it. We spiritualize His home because we can't imagine the sin that transpires in our homes took place in His. After all, everybody in Jesus' home knew who He was, right? Well, not really.

Jesus had brothers and sisters. In our terms today, they would be called half-brothers or half-sisters to be exact. They were brothers and sisters of the same mother but a different father. Have you considered this? Jesus grew up in a home where He was accepted by Joseph, the earthly father of that home, and was raised by him as his own. It was as if He had been adopted by Joseph.

The actual firstborn of Joseph and Mary was James! Jude came after, and then a few sisters followed him. Other than having Jesus as a son or brother, their home seemed like a normal Jewish home. They loved one another, and I'm sure they argued and had their own disagreements. Who knows, the children may have even had physical arguments!

Stay with me. I am going somewhere with this.

In order for Jesus to die on the cross for every sin and fulfill the justice of God as the perfect sacrifice, He had to bear the weight of the offenses, sins and heart wounds of His own earthly family. He had to live and experience a typical home life and familial relationships.

And like many of our own family experiences, His brothers and sisters weren't necessarily impressed by Him. In fact, they didn't believe in Him. They didn't believe in Jesus as Messiah (John 7:5). We can't find any of His family members at the cross save Mary, His mother. In this Man's darkest hours of His earthly journey, His brothers and sisters can't be found. Yet, we know later that James gets saved (1 Cor. 15:7). And, His brothers and sisters join the prayer meeting in the Upper Room with the disciples (Acts 1:14).

Imagine with me for a moment about what His childhood may have looked like. What was Jesus like as an eight year old? Maybe nobody wanted to play hide-and-seek with Him because He always found them! Perhaps that word of knowledge thing kicked in, and you know, it was game over. Whenever the kids on the block wanted to play king-of-the-hill, Jesus always won! I can imagine Mary's boys walking down the street some days, looking for their friends, while other mothers called their boys inside not allowing them to play with "the carpenter's brats"! I've been there! That's why it's easy for me to picture it happening to them.

Please humor me and see the possibilities with me. James

may have had to explain why Jesus always had to win. Time
and again, James may have tried to smooth things over until
one day he just couldn't take it anymore, so he blew up. In
the theater of my mind, I hear the conversation that may
have ensued.

"Why do you have to be the way you are, Jesus? Why
don't you just change? Who are you anyway? Who do you
think you are? God?"

No, I don't have any biblical foundation for this, just
family experience, like you do. From my experience, the cyn-
icism could have set in, and James's love would have started
to grow cold.

You know what? Being the family that raised Jesus
wouldn't have been easy. And when we as a family say *yes* to
Jesus, we start walking the road He walked, even in the hidden years—the years we don't see the Bible unpack for us.
We don't get to see them, but we know they had to have been
there. So we don't ever consider those years because we can't
prove them fully by Scripture. But He had to have faced some
of the universal realities of family life and of being different.

Furthermore, I grapple with the idea of how Mary and
Joseph led Jesus. For example, how would Joseph deal with
the insecurity of being a dad to...God?! Can you imagine
some of their conversations? They could have looked something like this.

"Now Jesus, *YHWH* says..."

"Abba, I know..."

"Oh, yeah...that's right, you probably do!"

How would you ever think you would have anything to
teach God? Oh, the potential for insecurity. Imagine Joseph
keeping the Passover with his family when the kids were
teenagers. Imagine Jesus' Bible reading that morning being
Isaiah 53—"and He was lead like a lamb to the slaughter..."
And then that night when Joseph would have cut the throat
of the lamb and Jesus' eyes open wide at all the blood. The

rest of the night He may have been quiet and serious, more to Himself than the usual tease (you know He teased!).

"Dale," you say, "you can't prove to me or tell me these things really happened!" My only defense would be simply this. Did Jesus grow up in a normal Jewish home? If you say *yes,* then the possibility of these things having happened is greater than you think.

So what's my point?

I think we know so very little of Jesus' hidden years because He has chosen in love "to cover over a multitude of sins" (James 5:20). You see, He had compassion for the home He lived in because He figured it out. He realized how difficult it must have been to stumble forward in life trying to raise Messiah. It shows us His humility as God. It reveals to us His ability to condescend to our estate, to our humanity—His ability to bring forth true love when all He had to deal with was human weakness and failure, IOUs and miles of "shoulda, coulda and wouldas." It shows us His ability to be merciful and takes us by the hand, pulling us out of our quicksand of "whatever" and planting us firmly on the right path.

Think of this: no James at the cross, post resurrection Jesus appeared to James (1 Cor. 15:7) and the next we see of James he was in the Upper Room (Acts 1:14). After that, we find James pastoring the church in Jerusalem (Acts 15).

What happened? As I said in chapter one, mercy won! Jesus took James by the hand and led him out of his spiritual poverty, helping him see the reality and grace of Messiah in His resurrected body.

When, after all those years growing up together, James touches the mercy given by Jesus, he turns his life over to his brother's leadership. With deep gratitude, he moves forward in his life, thankful his past is covered in love—thankful Somebody who was merciful understood the nature of the stumbling in this one particular family.

Jesus is still merciful and able to cover over a multitude of sins. He's able and willing to redeem the lost. We can attest to His doing that for us. No, we may not have deserved mercy, but we all needed it! (We need it yet today and will need it in all our tomorrows.) And we all must learn to be merciful, to give what we've received from Him. We can't give what we don't have. Only when we've been the recipients of such mercy can we do mercy, not condemning the guiltless. Jesus learned mercy. He learned how to communicate mercy, and we must too.

CHAPTER 5

Tongues of Mercy

"If anyone does not stumble in word, he is a perfect man,
able also to bridle the whole body" (James 3:2).

I used to be a middle school teacher. What a wild ride! It was great! I never really knew from day to day what to expect. There's nothing more exquisite and confusing than the middle school mind. As a teacher, I knew what homework was and dispensed a lot of it as "extra practice," at least that's how I used to sell it.

This year the Lord has shown me *my homework*. He has called me to battle for a tongue of mercy. I'm enthralled by the opportunity though I'm trembling from the fear of the Lord. As I've stepped into this challenge, I'm actually in pain over the condition of my tongue because of how it's revealing the motivations of my heart. James 3, however, helps me.

In this chapter, James gives us three metaphors that negatively express the effects of the tongue when not controlled. He speaks of a bit in a horse's mouth, the rudder of a ship and the spark of fire that sets a forest ablaze.

I've read this chapter again and again with the Lord so kindly giving me tender impressions that are moving my heart. He actually is showing me that these metaphors used by James can be seen as a kind invitation rather than a threatening rebuke. Let me explain.

First, James speaks of the tongue as being like a bit in a horse's mouth. With this bit connected to the reigns and bridle, the rider can control the power of an obedient horse. Here's our first invitation.

With us as obedient horses, Jesus as our rider and a bit in our mouths, He may have full control of *what* comes out of our mouths and *when* it comes out. Power can be released, and this power may be used for His purposes.

With a bit, the full power of the horse is controlled and released at the will of the rider. That is a very positive metaphor. I can give myself to that. I can respond positively to that invitation.

Next, James employs the picture of a ship driven by great winds yet steered by such a small rudder directing the ship where to go. With Holy Spirit filling the sails and captaining the ship, that rudder can be used to direct the course of not only individuals, but it can steer nations too.

Oh, the potential for the release of Holy Spirit through the tongue! With clarity of direction during the storms of life, the submitted tongue can obey the orders of its Captain. That sounds very enticing to me also.

In Revelation 11, certain men speak clear prophetic direction to the Church, to Israel and to the nations of the earth during the Great Tribulation. These obviously have done their homework with their tongue. They're the Two Witnesses who release powerful signs and wonders. I see them like James's horse with bit and bridle in their mouths under the control of Christ, and I see them like James's ship with their tongues being the rudders that clearly direct the earth in the end-time storms.

Lastly, James uses the great forest that is kindled with a little fire. Consider two points with me here. I believe the great forest to be the people of the earth. When Jesus healed a man who was blind, at first the blind man said, "I see men like trees, walking" (Mark 8:24). There is a great forest on the earth that only needs a match to start it burning. At first we may think it's bad for a fire to consume the forest. However, and this is my opinion, the fire is going to come one way or the other. It will come from either the anti-Christ or Jesus Christ. So who would you rather be on fire for when Jesus returns? Wisdom tells us we should be on fire for Christ.

My other point is that in James 1 we are told of the Father of lights. He, of course, is speaking of our heavenly Father. Daniel saw Him as the Ancient of Days, sitting on a throne of fire (Dan. 7). Now watch this!

Lights here in the Greek text is *phos*. We get the word *phosphorus* from this Greek root word. The nature of phosphorus is very peculiar. Under water it doesn't extinguish. It's dormant there. Expose it to oxygen, and it explodes; it burns. Like the Word of God hidden in your heart, when mixed with oxygen (breath), it comes out of your mouth and has explosive properties! It starts fires in the hearts of men.

Getting back to the Greek root word *phos*, it's important to understand the word means two things: (1) unquenchable and (2) unkindled.

The two meanings for *phos*, then, define God, the Ancient of Days, as a fire that cannot be quenched and that was unkindled.

Who lit God's heart on fire? No one for God is a consuming fire!

With Jesus in control of the reigns of your mouth, with Holy Spirit as the Captain of your ship controlling its rudder and the Father of lights igniting your tongue, you have the potential to be one of His fiery end-time messengers.

But remember, school's in session! If you do your homework well, He will prepare you.

Like I used to tell my middle schoolers, "Don't cheat yourself! Don't cut corners! Stay in school!"

If you do the work in the Father's school, you'll be rewarded.

Before we close out this chapter, I want to give you your first homework assignment. I ask that you consider with me the Day of Pentecost. Remember the events of that day? Men speaking with new tongues that looked like fire resting on their heads (Acts 2)?

Peter, the one disciple who struggled with foot-in-mouth disease while Jesus was on the earth, gave one of the greatest sermons human ears have ever heard. Connecting the outpouring of Holy Spirit to Joel, he made it clear that even today we await words from men and women of God that will shake heavenly bodies, ignite fires of passion in the human heart and direct the final judgments on the wicked anti-Christ regime.

If that is what we're headed for, then what is our homework now as we say *yes* to God's potential for our tongues?

It's a sobering reality yet the possibilities seem endless... tongues that speak like angels and have love, men who prophesy causing demons to flee as light breaks in and singers and musicians who shift principalities with the heavenly oracles sung around the throne of God.

Solomon was right, "Death and life are in the power of the tongue..." (Prov. 18:31). Of course, Jesus was right too when He said that out of the overflow of the heart the mouth speaks (Luke 6:45).

I'm excited, and I'm terrified!

You and I have much homework to do, and I think I know how we can start. Let me leave you with this thought.

Zacharias, the father of John the Baptist, was ministering in the temple at the altar of incense. He was adding incense when Gabriel, the messenger from the Lord, appeared to him and spoke to him regarding the life of his son.

Zacharias heard the message and questioned what the angel said. Disturbed by the unbelief of the priest's heart, the angel called for a nine-month silent fast! Ouch!

Zacharias came out of the temple unable to speak until he named his son. Upon receiving his voice back, he declared the mandate of the next generation who would prepare the way of the Lord.

It's hard for us to imagine and strange for us to consider. There are many types of fasts in the Bible, but this silent fast by Zacharias, though imposed by an angel, gave this priest nine months to prepare to announce the emergence of a new generation.

I think this is where we should start. As strange as it sounds, and as feeble as it may seem, I call us to exercise the one "human right" most of us rarely employ *the right to remain silent!*

We should start there, and the Lord will do the rest. He'll grant us tongues of mercy that can set the world ablaze for His glory. But first, we must face the wilderness of His mercy.

CHAPTER 6

The Wilderness of Mercy

"'Blessed are those who hunger and thirst...'"
(Matt. 5:6).

One summer while visiting my parents in Whitehorse, Yukon, Northern Canada, we took a drive to Skagway, Alaska. The landscape was spectacular and unique to the region. Pine forests, fields with windblown fireweed, rugged mountains, freezing cold rivers and riveting turquoise lakes.

Abba, Father, I thought to myself, *You made this just for me to see!*

As I was drinking in the incredible vistas before me, we crested a hill on the narrow highway and came upon the Carcross Desert. The Carcross Desert in the Yukon Territory of Canada covers an area of approximately 640 acres and is the smallest desert in the world. Across this desert you will find a unique mixture of vegetation and sand dunes due to the dry climate and extremely strong winds that sweep across the region.

As we came over the hill, I was shocked into silence, especially in light of my meditation at the time... *You made this just for me to see!*

"Stop the car!" I called out.

I got out of the car and stood on top of one of the sand dunes in amazement at the utter barrenness of the vast land-scape in front of me. Though not large, it was bigger than I, that's for sure, and was very intimidating. I suddenly became thirsty, probably because of what the desert represented.

My heart was wide-open that day I think because of the other landscapes I was drinking in. Then this! How do you drink from the beauty of a desert wilderness? How do you look at a barren wasteland, sand, a few cactus, some scrub bushes and call it beautiful?

The Sahara it was not. I had seen the Sahara. With the heat coming off the sand, the sun baking what little vegeta-tion there was—I just thought, *How does anything survive out here?*

Life is like a barren wilderness. I mean, when I look at the glories waiting to be revealed to us, this place right now—this life—is a barren desert! And, this narrow road we walk upon because we love Jesus makes this present age seem even more like a desolate wasteland.

Psalm 90:10–12 tells us, "The days of our lives are sev-enty years; and if by reason of strength they are eighty years, yet their boast is only labor and sorrow; for it is soon cut off, and we fly away.... So teach us to number our days, that we may gain a heart of wisdom." Moses wrote this psalm, and he was right. When I look at the days of my life, I'm chal-lenged with the futility of a life lived devoid of God.

Without proper perspective and point of view on this life, I lack the necessary wisdom for this brief pilgrimage. Without this understanding, I can become lost and parched in the wilderness of life. Yet with all my heart I tell you there is no better school for God's ministers than the wilderness.

Speaking about God's school in the desert, I'm reminded again of John the Baptist. I've always been intrigued by his story. I know I referred in the last chapter to the angelic an-nouncement of his birth and his father's response, but have you ever considered his life?

We think of his ministry and the thousands who were born again and baptized into a new kingdom at his hands. We think of his clothes of camel's hair and diet of locust and wild honey. We think of his words to the masses, to the Pharisees, to Jesus and to Herod, the latter being the ones that got him killed.

But have you ever considered his early years? What did the pre-ministry years of John look like? Now that's something to consider!

Looking back prior to John's birth to Zacharias and Elizabeth, we read of Zach who ministered at the altar when an angel spoke to him regarding the life of his son. We discussed before how Zach doubted it and was sent on a nine-month-long silent fast.

I'm sure Elizabeth found that refreshing—a husband who couldn't speak!

Anyway, John was born nine months later, and at the day of his dedication and naming, the family argued about just what his name should be. There was no one else in the family line named John, so they wanted a different name selected.

Elizabeth said *no*, and Zach still couldn't talk. I bet she was mad at her husband and thought, *This is all your fault!*

No matter what she thought, Zach wrote that the child's name would be John. And BAM! Zach's mouth was opened, so he was able to prophesy of the generation in which John lived. He prophesied about the coming Messiah and the work of his son to prepare the way for this expected One of Israel.

Zach's prophecy to John's generation reminds me of the new thing I see the Lord doing in this hour. For many of us, this new thing has never been manifested in our family history before, but that doesn't mean it's not of God. It just means it's new!

In order for us to call forth the next generation, we'll

need several months of silence, some deep heart work and the willingness to risk our all for the sake of an emerging age group that will prepare the way of the Lord.

Oh, and one final thing we'll need is the courage to plunge that generation into wilderness places, to call them to believe being in the wilderness is wisdom for a future coming day and ask them to believe that such a barren place is beautiful.

We'll need to take them there ourselves and raise them there if need be. It might mean our work is taking them to the wilderness and being seen by them and others as unloving or unmerciful. But it's in the wilderness, not necessarily on the psychologist's couch, that a generation will learn to unpack all the pain of loneliness, despair and trauma from rough roads and wayward highways.

Luke 1:80 tells us, and this is my paraphrase, that Zach looked at the prevailing culture of his day, even the religious culture, and decided it would not have the ability to prepare his son for the calling on the boy's life. So he moved him to wilderness places until it was time for John to enter ministry.

In the wilderness, there is only one voice—the voice of God! There are also cackling hyenas that represent the countless millions who say such sacrifices are foolish.

In the wilderness places, all self-indulgent, envious self-seeking is purged in the fires of trial and difficulty. All fleshly desires are exchanged for the deep loving zeal of God as He empties us of carnal ways and fills us with Himself.

Friends, if we are willing to take it, the wilderness, though a lonely place at times, prepares us for future plans written only in the heart of God.

The wilderness might mean seclusion but not necessarily. The wilderness is not just dry desert regions. There are many who claim to be in deserted dry places, but really they're in confusion regarding life and God.

The wilderness place can be literal or figurative by definition. We already know what a literal wilderness is. I described that at the beginning of this chapter. It's a physical place that's out-of-the-way, a place where there are no others to bother us or tether us to life's lustful pursuits.

Moses was familiar with such a place. But one day while in the wilderness, Moses saw something very different. I'm sure he had seen many burning bushes in his life. Hundreds, I guess! Remember where he lived. He lived in the Sinai wilderness. It was a hot, arid place. The heat would have caused dry bushes to self-combust, almost exploding with fire. No, he had seen many bushes that burned with fire.

What was so special about this one? The bush burned *but* was not consumed! The fire didn't consume the shrub. It stood only as a witness that something different was going on. It was this difference that spoke to the hunger for God inside Moses. *How could a bush burn and not be consumed?* he wondered.

God was speaking Moses' language! The wilderness had been Moses' friend. He was fashioned by God in the desert place. And, when it was time to give him his mandate for freeing Jewish slaves in Egypt, God spoke to him in a way that would catch his attention.

A bush that burned but was not consumed meant a man could burn with the fire of God and not be consumed! I believe Moses was the Bible's first burning man!

Elijah, too, was a burning man, as were the prophets. These all were men and women who burned with the Word of God shut up in their bones. They carried the burden of the Lord. And they all were very familiar with the wilderness.

The wilderness can be figurative as well. Daniel was not in a literal wilderness but in the very heart of civilization in his time. He was in Babylon, the most powerful city with the most powerful kings of the earth. Daniel was in a *figurative* wilderness, one complete with every trap and temptation known in the world.

Daniel chose early not to live by the appetites of this

figurative wilderness place. Though he was in the midst of a pompous, self-indulgent culture surrounded with every temptation known to man—food from the king's table, position and power, influence and wealth—he considered himself in a desert place compared to being in the temple of God. He had heard the prophets, seen Josiah's revival, known the temple of God and His ways and heard the stories of His powerful acts.

Daniel had everything at his fingertips, every comfort he could want, but was in a foreign land that caged him. He was not free to leave his cultural barren wasteland devoid of the truths of God. He was captured in the fruitless wasteland of self-indulgence, self-seeking, endless power plays motivated by envy and mountains of political intrigue.

Perhaps you find yourself alone in a wilderness surrounded by the prevailing culture of our day. It too is a culture of self-indulgence and political intrigue where people constantly jockey for position and power. Ours is a dog-eat-dog world so selfish and narcissistic that it defines a wilderness or desert as five-thousand square-feet of house with ten bedrooms and an outdoor pool overlooking a golf course somewhere!

Or maybe the wilderness is your bedroom Bible school at home where you sit alone for hours with the Scriptures and your guitar. Your wilderness may be the constant noes you've uttered to so-called friends who have invited you to parties meant to satisfy the lonely ache for fellowship deep inside of you. Your wilderness may even be the constant moving of your family from one place to another and the disruption of your friendship circles and loss of community. I know some whose wilderness is another church meeting devoid of the presence and power of God with no other perceivable options. Maybe like them, you're in the desert place where you're driven by your hunger for God yet remain insatiable. Oh, the paradox of a God who invites you to the wilderness to eat and then slays you with hunger and thirst (Hosea 2:3)

This place, this wilderness place, is the wisdom and mercy of God. It is how He prepares messengers for His purposes. It is how He prepares those who will announce His coming and prepare the way for the people to move toward Him instead of away from Him.

If you can receive it, God has been and is being very kind to you.

The wilderness places are the only places where we meet God at a deeper level. He inhabits every place, but few go to the wilderness due to its discomfort. See, He's waiting there so that He might burn away the desire for the false comforts the world offers that do not really comfort at all.

He calls us to the wilderness places, whether literal or figurative, to make us burn with what causes Him to burn. We become bushes that are on fire but are not consumed. We become burning men and women, burning and shining lamps, prepared and ready for the service He grants to us.

These final hours of human history will call for the deepest and greatest responses in the human heart so as to navigate them successfully. These godly responses are not pre-programmed into our DNA. No, they're only stirred in the wilderness. His journey for us always takes us through the wilderness places. He's forging vessels of honor. Will we cooperate with His processes?

If you want to live for God and love God without fail in these coming end-times, you must first face the wilderness. It's unavoidable! It's uncomfortable! And it seems uninhabitable! But it's His mercy you'll find there as you cry out to Him.

CHAPTER 7

Cry for Mercy

"When Jesus departed from there, two blind men followed Him, crying out and saying, 'Son of David, have mercy on us!'" (Matt. 9:27).

G od's heart is vulnerable to us. The cry coming from the human soul moves the very core of His being. When He hears a sincere cry, He *has* to answer it!

The Gospels record stories of those who cried out to Jesus using His title, "Son of David." I've found an interesting fact: All those in the Bible who cried out for mercy using this name—Son of David—every one of them were healed and/or delivered. I mean, every time, the cry of "Jesus, Son of David, have mercy" rang out, someone was changed forever.

David, Christ's ancestor, learned mercy and was merciful himself. David's mercy impacted generations. As the Scripture tells us in Exodus 20:5, God is jealous. Furthermore, the text informs us that He visits "the iniquity of the fathers upon the children to the third or fourth generations of those who hate" Him, *but* He shows "*mercy* to thousands, to those who love" Him and keep His commandments (v. 6, emphasis added). Some versions of the latter part of the verse read that He shows mercy to *a thousand generations* of those who love

Him. I like to look at it this way, that Jesus saw the family photo album of His forefather, King David, and decided to learn from his life. Maybe those who cried out to the Son of David saw some family resemblance themselves.

There are three examples of cries for mercy that come to my mind. Two are from the Gospels and one from the Old Testament. Let's look at the one from the Old Testament first.

In the history of Israel, during the time of the judges, the people went from one extreme to the other. One moment they served the Lord, and the next they bowed before idols and played the harlot (to use King James English). On one such occasion, God handed them over to their enemies to be taught a lesson.

Judges 10 shows us a specific time where the Philistines and Ammonites rose up against Israel. The people groaned and cried out. God spoke to them through a prophet, telling them to cry out to their mute idol gods who couldn't deliver them. In this instance, the people cried out for help, even putting away their idols. What happened next is classic God!

Verses 15–16 say, "And the children of Israel said to the Lord, 'We have sinned! Do to us whatever seems best to You; only deliver us this day, we pray.' So they put away the foreign gods from among them and served the Lord. *And His soul could no longer endure the misery of Israel,*" (emphasis added).

Can you believe what you just read? God's soul couldn't take it anymore. He couldn't endure their miserable cries. That fact alone should cause us to wake up. We think the New Testament nullifies the Old, but it does nothing of the sort! In this story, God used wicked nations to discipline His people and turn them back to Himself. *This* displayed His mercy! We need to understand His heart even in our generation.

God wants to be the answer to the cry of every human

heart! He loves being the cavalry, the knight in shining armor, the SWAT team and the Navy Seals (sorry, Army Rangers). When a sincere cry followed by clear action goes out, God answers for His heart melts at our cry for mercy. The groan of the people touched the groan in God's heart, and the result was deliverance!

Another example of God's responding to our cries for mercy is the story of the two blind men that begins at Matthew 9:27. Only a few verses before, Jesus raised a girl from the dead. He was in the process of moving on when these two loud blind guys latched onto Him. As the crowd passed by their way, they started crying out, "Son of David, have mercy on us!"

They didn't cry out, "Jesus, Son of Joseph!" Neither did they say, "Jesus, Son of God!" Why Son of David?

Easy! Probably the greatest revelation of God that David trusted in and lived out was his belief in God's mercy. David was so sure of God's mercy that he ran into His arms instead of away from Him in shame. This revelation so impacted his family line that, down through the generations—right to his son Jesus—many were living in the generational blessing of this revelation of God.

I believe we can see God's point in these stories. He wants us living in the sure mercies—the faithful mercies—given to David. God wants us confident in His mercy. So many times David appealed to the mercy of God and got it because he knew it was his lifeline. David knew the living God was merciful.

I've had to cry out for the mercy of God throughout my life. We all have. But for many, when we run into God, it looks more like the unmerciful servant in Matthew 18. We aren't really looking for mercy; instead, we want more time to pay back a debt that we have no hope of settling. Even when the master in the story offers mercy, the servant doesn't get it.

You know, there are just times when we need to be loud

in our prayers and requests. We need to let our prayers come from our guts, expressing the deepest cries of our hearts. Jesus did it, the apostles did it, and men and women in the Old Testament did it. And as we've seen evidenced in the Bible, God responds to the cries of the oppressed.

One final story from the Gospels touches my heart. It's the story of the Canaanite woman in Matthew 15 who came to Jesus begging for help with her demonized daughter. Two things really get me about this story. The first thing is that she would unashamedly ask for help, and the second is the way Jesus treated her.

The Canaanite woman had to push past a lot of stumbling blocks to get to the mercy of God resident in the heart of Jesus. She faced three tests, and I love what Jesus did here with her. I think His aim in treating her the way He did was to strengthen her faith in His mercy, thereby strengthening her faith that she could ask God anytime for it and expect help.

Let's look at how He handled her.

She cried out to Him, "Have mercy on me, O Lord, Son of David! My daughter is severely demon-possessed!" (v. 22). Her desperate plea was met with dead silence. Jesus said nothing. Have you ever had your cries for mercy met with silence? I have. It's brutal on the heart and great for maturing love in Christ.

Not only was Jesus quiet, but not one of the disciples advocated for her. On the contrary, they asked Jesus to send her away. The disciples interpreted Jesus' silence as the non-verbal cue to get rid of her. She had no apparent allies—no one seemingly present to respond to her request.

Finally, when Jesus did speak, it was to His disciples' comments about sending her away. And the answer He gave them was downright offensive to her. He said, "I was not sent except to the lost sheep of the house of Israel" (v. 24).

What? He would not respond to her because she was a Gentile?

Jesus' statement did not stop her. She continued to press. She came close and worshipped him. Imagine that. The Greek tells us she prostrated herself and yelped like a little dog cuddling up to its master. That's no ordinary worship!

I'm amazed at Jesus' ability to hold on and not melt at the sight of such self-deprecation. Guess what Jesus did next? He straight up offended her. He said, "You don't take the children's bread and give it to the dogs" (v. 26).

From all external vantage points, Jesus looked as though He were disrespecting her. It was quite the opposite, however. He was helping her more by not giving her the mercy at her initial request. He wanted her rooted and grounded in the strength of His mercy.

Her persistence was strengthened and faith empowered as she replied to Him, "Yes, Lord, yet even the little dogs eat the crumbs which fall from the master's table" (v. 27).

"O woman, great is your faith! Let it be to you as you desire," He told her (v. 28). And her daughter received healing right then and there.

Recently I've looked at places in my own life and said, "God, only You can move this. Mercy, I need your mercy!" We are powerless to free ourselves from years of habits and paradigms that need to change. We need His mercy. We need Him to take us by the hand and lead us out. We need Him to strengthen us.

But as He leads us out, He often chooses to do things in such a way to strengthen our faith in His mercy. He's training something in us so, when we are not around Him, our hearts can reach back into what He did previously and live out of it again. He's helping us deal with every obstacle, knowing it will strengthen us and make us determined to find His mercy.

In His mercy, I believe Jesus is about to do this in the church. Many are stuck in their ways and want out. Long ago, these ways seemed to be wise but have proven over time

to be the contrary. Now that a generation stands looking at
what God has promised and knows how not to pursue it,
they're hungry for change while still bound to old patterns,
habits and paradigms.

He is only a cry away.

But...don't get offended with Him when He's silent at
first. He's not looking to keep us as children. He wants to
move us into maturity.

He may treat many like this poor Canaanite woman. If
they learn to respond as she—"Yes, Lord, I know you don't
give the children's bread to dogs. But the dogs get a few
crumbs from their master's table"—they will get her reward.

We need to persist. We need cry out to Him again and
again until He answers us, bringing us to a place of faith and
strength in His mercy.

CHAPTER 8

The Boundaries of Mercy

*"For the LORD brings a charge against the inhabitants of the
land: 'There is no truth or mercy or knowledge
of God in the land'" (Hosea 4:1).*

*H*ave you ever considered that the matchless, limitless,
infinite, eternal God has set clear boundaries for us?
He's limitless while we're limited. He says He's the Alpha and
the Omega, the beginning and the end, but can anyone tell me
where His beginning is or show me His end?

Herein rests the tension. If this loving God has made man
in His image and likeness, and God is infinite and limitless,
then why does He enclose us in the limitations of our bodies
or surround us with time and space? Why does He give us
such limits and then call us to love Him? This inner tension
is the root of many of the greatest battles you and I will wage
on the earth, this side of the Second Coming!

For centuries, humankind has pushed against these
boundaries. Casting off restraint, we have sought higher en-
lightenment, greater powers, religious perfection and military
dominance. Even today, we hate, and I mean *hate*, human
weakness. Believe me, hate is not too strong of a word.

Think of this. God delivers His people from Egypt with

51

a mighty hand. I mean the light show and fireworks were amazing, were they not? His sole design was to have them come to His mountain and worship Him. Moses got them to the mountain, and God started to set boundaries! There they were in a major *freedom* mode, and God set boundaries! What was that about?

God commanded Moses to build a tabernacle in order for the people to relate to Him. The first thing He tells him to do is put up a boundary—an outer wall of goatskins! This God is so paradoxical.

Later in biblical history, David set out to restore the ark of God to the nation's capital. He made a cart and started to move. Next thing he knew, the oxen stumbled, the ark tipped, Uzziah reached out and touched the ark, resulting in a billion volts of electricity taking him out right there!

How is it that we reach for God, like Uzziah reached to stabilize the ark, but we can't touch Him? What is God doing with us?

Boundaries!

Why?

In the end, we want God made in our image. We reach for Him, wanting Him to be what we want Him to be rather than embracing Him and who He actually is in His totality. God wants us for who we are, and He is looking for a people who will take Him for who He is!

In the end, anything made by our hands will fail. Think of it, for it's our history. We make our own images and build our own concepts of God, worship them, and then they fail. Offended, we accuse Him of not loving us and of sabotaging our lives.

God wants us to search Him out. He loves treasure hunts, and He makes Himself the pot of gold at the end of the rainbow of mercy! Without His boundaries and game of hide-and-seek, we'd just say, "Give me the gold," and walk away from the Giver of the gold. If we're honest, most of the time we see Him as the means to an end—to greater anointing, greater riches, better cars, more honor from men. All this is immaturity. However, He *is* the end! He *is* the goal of life. He *is* willing to work with this immature love but only in His way. And what is His way?

His way is through boundaries!

Hosea the prophet was familiar with God's way. God commanded him to take Gomer, an adulterous woman, as his wife. He told Hosea ahead of time that she was going to be unfaithful to him. Sounds rough, doesn't it? But God was after something. He wanted Israel to see a virtual picture of her relationship with Him.

In essence He said, "Israel, you are a harlot! You are not my wife. Put away your harlotries!" (Hosea 2:2). Wow! Okay, that was direct!

Israel, like Gomer, was running to and fro, chasing after other images of the knowledge of God—images built by her own hands. All the while, she ignored the true revelation of God. As our opening verse for this chapter tells us, no truth, mercy or knowledge of God was in her land (4:1).

This was the Lord's charge against the nation. He was accusing them of not manifesting the truth about Him. He basically said, "You don't know Me. You are running after other options. I love mercy. I honor truth. The knowledge of Me is the beginning of wisdom. Real life, eternal life is knowing Me. But you are poor, blind, naked and wretched!"

So there was Gomer, the picture of the nation of Israel. She was chasing after her other lovers and adorning herself in a seductive way to capture the gaze of the other men in the city. And then God instructed Hosea on how He was going to remove the harlot from Israel. This plan He gave to Hosea to use with Gomer. What was God's plan?

Using boundaries!

God planned to hedge her in, to set her within boundaries. Gomer experienced some painful things that did not allow her to find her other lovers. She turned left and hit a wall. She turned right and hit another wall. There was no place for her to go except in one direction and that was back toward her husband's door!

Boundary number one, her access to her other options, was removed. She couldn't get to her other lovers, and her other lovers couldn't get to her.

Included in this, God sang to Israel about her true identity as His wife. He spoke to her and reminded her that she belonged to Him. He revealed that in relationship to Him she would find her true identity and the fullness of mercy. Choose Him, and she would get mercy and find the truth of who she was.

This song and this relationship were restored in the wilderness of trouble. Her only hope for survival and true love were found as trouble made her face her broken images of God. She was offered the option of mercy in the midst of trouble, but the question begged answering: Would she humble herself and take it?

Boundary number two, the wilderness of trouble, provided the only hope for mercy. Here Gomer was abandoned. Her other lovers didn't want to come to her aid. She was forsaken, rejected. She was left with only one who would love her in this lion's den, only one who would take her back in her broken condition.

In the story, Hosea went to the marketplace and bought back his wife. Like any other man looking for a prostitute, he went to negotiate for her. He paid money for her though, by rights of their marriage covenant, she belonged to him—he had open access to her. He paid her debt, wrapped his cloak around her and took her home. He restored her purity and wholesomeness through another boundary.

Boundary number three was they would share no sexual intimacy. She was forgiven of adultery. She had been redeemed. It was mercy that brought her home. And, please hear me, it was mercy that withheld from her for a period of time so she could demonstrate she had received forgiveness and was willing to restore trust.

I believe forgiveness and trust are two different things. Forgiveness is a principle we activate every day from our free will. Hosea forgave and demonstrated that forgiveness by restoring her and paying for her return home. That was showing mercy. And that is a picture of our Jesus forgiving us (Hosea 3:1–3).

However, trust is earned. Trust is one of the most vulnerable and fragile places in the human heart. Ask any man or woman who has been broken and betrayed by a wayward spouse, he or she will tell you I'm speaking the truth.

I realize that Hosea's boundary was a prophetic picture to the nation that Israel would not have a king for a while, but in his relationship with his wife, this was a clear boundary for Gomer. Now that she was home, she had some work to do.

Hear me, and let me be very clear. She did not have to earn his love again. She had his love; he proved it by buying her back from the marketplace. Likewise, we do not have to earn the love of our dear Jesus. No! No! No! Earning His love, now *that* would be legalism!

No, she had his love as we have the love of Jesus every day. He can't love us more tomorrow than He did today, and He won't love us more today than He did yesterday. Why? Because He is always wholehearted. His love has been fully poured out and is always given wholeheartedly and completely!

Gomer needed the time to activate her will and do the work of building trust again.

The foundation of our relationship with Jesus is love. This relationship, however, is not a passive one full of empty promises and little demonstration. No, there are so many places in Scripture that prove this point.

Adam was given a work to do. He cultivated a garden for encountering God.

Noah was given a task to demonstrate his faith and trust in God's judgment plan. He built an ark.

Abraham was given a task. He obediently offered his son as a sacrifice to God (though God gave the son back to his father).

Moses had a work to do. He delivered Israel from Egypt.

John the Baptist was born with a job description. He prepared the way of the Lord.

Peter, James and John were personally given their work. Jesus told them to feed His sheep.

The disciples had jobs from the beginning. They followed Jesus when everybody else walked in another direction.

The apostle Paul was called by God to a specific people. He preached to the Gentiles, telling them to work out their salvation.

James, the Lord's brother, had his task too. He showed his faith by his works!

What am I telling you?

Jesus accepted the boundaries and limitation placed upon Him in His first advent. As our example, He took those boundaries and limitations and called them God's mercy strategy for Him while on the earth. On the cross, He turned those boundaries from the bitter screams of others into His love language offered to Father.

While many in this life clamor for rights and freedoms, few reach for the responsibilities of the freedoms that the cross calls for. I believe we will be *judged* for our response to the plumb line of the cross and *rewarded* for our love offering made every day before the throne of God.

I think the Lord is looking for restraint in this hour of human history. All through the ages, mankind has been trying to cast off restraint. David told us about it in Psalm 2:1–3, and it's still manifesting in this hour with greater intensity.

He said, "Why do the nations rage, and the peoples plot a vain thing? The kings of the earth set themselves, and the rulers take counsel together against the Lord and against His Anointed, saying, 'Let us break their bonds in pieces, and cast away their cords from us.'"

Jesus called us all to take up the cross, deny ourselves and follow Him. What does it profit us if we gain all the freedoms in the world but forfeit our souls on Judgment Day (Luke 9:3)?

Gomer's and Israel's boundaries were made clear by the mercy of God. I think our boundaries are clear too. I think we find them in the Sermon on the Mount. As I see it, each of us has been given a garden to tend. I see the Beatitudes as eight fruit trees that we cultivate for the Lord because of love (Matt. 5:3–11). We are to pull the weeds, the toxins of sin (Matt. 5:21–48), that try to spoil our gardens. We have tools given to us with which to tend our garden—tools of prayer, fasting, generosity, blessing our enemies and faithful service (Matt. 6).

With these boundaries, grace from above rests upon us. We build our houses firmly on the bedrock of Jesus Christ Himself. Jesus held Himself to these trusted boundaries not in a religious way but because of love. It was His gift before Father. It restored Father's trust in man again. Finally, a Man came who loved Father simply, clearly, freely and all within the boundaries set by Father's design!

I am calling myself and the body of Christ to return again to the yoke of Jesus. And His yoke is easy and His burden light. I am calling myself and the body of Christ to dispense with the fight for freedoms that are not freedoms but lusts that actually war against our souls. I am asking, with deep humility, that we all grow up in love and start giving back to the Lord the love He deserves. It starts by our accepting His sure boundaries that carry His grace.

I am calling us all to return again to the sacred things of

Jesus' heart. I am challenging us all with a sacred charge to pray daily, fast weekly, speak boldly, do justly, give extravagantly, live holy and lead diligently. Let's do this all within the boundaries of His mercy, motivated by the seal of His love.

CHAPTER 9

Unsanctified Mercy

"In those days, there was no king in Israel; everyone did what was right in his own eyes" (Judg. 21:25).

"Now it came to pass, in the days when the judges ruled, that there was a famine in the land" (Ruth 1:1).

The boundaries of God are necessary. They help us identify *unsanctified mercy* or *false mercy*. Though this is not a biblical term, we see it in operation in the church in the Western world and in the lives of people in the Bible.

False or unsanctified mercy is extending mercy to that which God *is not* granting mercy (Rom. 9:15). The danger of unsanctified mercy is that we may begin to presume that God will never exercise judgment and will only show mercy. Additionally, we may stop asking God what He thinks about our lives, thereby becoming fearless of His judgment and wrath for our wickedness and sin. All of this denies Him the opportunity to speak true mercy.

Just in case you don't think you're susceptible to unsanctified mercy, please allow me to tell you how I've seen it creep into my own thought life at times. You see, I've been victimized by unsanctified mercy. It has allowed me to think, for example:

- we're going in the right direction in America and Western civilization.
- the lack of authority in my prayer life is acceptable.
- there are still many years before I have to face the major storms of this generation.

Unsanctified mercy is like a vaporous, poisonous fog, allowing me to nestle a little too closely to the grievous patterns of sin in my life that I wink at every day. This unrighteous form of mercy let's me cry out, "Grace, grace, Lord," instead of, "Kill it, Lord!"

Unsanctified mercy is what we employ each time we try to talk our friends or family out of their repentance or convictions, not understanding that God meant for us to humble ourselves too!

And it was unsanctified mercy that led Elimelech and Naomi from their homeland and inheritance toward the greener pastures of Moab where enemies of Israel, God's people, lived.

Let's consider Elimelech for a moment. His name in Hebrew means *My God is King*. What an awesome name! I mean, imagine having that stamped on the DNA of your heart. You would think this man would constantly be driven by the fact His God *is* King.

Yet, think about it. Elimelech was not living with that inner revelation of God manifesting in his corporate reality!

We share the same weakness with Elimelech. We always look for the greener pastures. By nature we are creatures that seek comfort from the tensions of our souls and stomachs. Seldom do we turn our eyes heavenward and cry out for understanding regarding the internal fights that take place in our hearts each day.

Read the last verse in Judges 21 (v. 25) and then the very next verse in the Bible (Ruth 1:1). You'll see an astounding truth setting the stage for Elimelech's decisions. Judges 21:25 tells us that there wasn't a king in Israel then, so everyone "did what was right in his own eyes." And when we read the opening of the next book, Ruth, we read during the days of the judges there was a famine in the land. This famine caused Elimelech, Naomi and their two sons to go and dwell in Moab.

Judges clearly tells us that the general decision-making patterns of Elimelech's day were a type of anarchy that we see being repeated today. There is no kingly authority in our land today, so we do what we think is right in our own eyes. We've become disjointed and lonely. We make independent decisions with little or no input from the ones who love us and know God's heart for us. We've grown accustomed to the lack of leadership in our nations. And we've settled for that fact and learned to live with it. We're looking everywhere else for leadership but not to the right Person—not to Jesus (Ps. 23:1; John 10:11, 14). Elimelech did the same thing.

I can also imagine that, perhaps if he did appeal to God, there was silence for a season to test the construct of his inner soul. Would he persevere until he got an answer? Imagine this with me for a moment.

I can imagine he thought in his quiet time, *My God is King!* He left the comfort of his personal prayer closet with the love of the heavenly King still soothing his heart. He stepped outside into the searing Judean summer heat. It was a million degrees Fahrenheit with those dry, scorching sirocco winds. The crops disintegrated in the fields, the cattle just sat there lowing for water, and his sons cut open the dusty ground knowing it was useless to plow. Then and there he decided, *In Moab they have green grass and a king. We're outta here!*

"And they loaded up the truck and moved to Beverly!" as the TV theme song says (pun absolutely intended).

What just happened?

The true implanted desire of a man's heart, given to him by God as an individual, collided with the truth of his corporate setting. God does this to us in mercy. He does it to help us see the truth resident in the heart of our communities.

Elimelech was bursting to see the truth of God revealed on the earth, God's choice for King. This was a true desire from God, but Elimelech may have been bitten with a deeper sin pattern just like his countrymen. I'm sure he was hungry, and hunger can drive people to do all kinds of things. But when we consider the last verse in Judges, I also believe it was possible for Elimelech to think what so many others were thinking at that time, *I'm just going to do what I think is best, and that's it.*

Seeking to comfort the desire of his heart, he abandoned his land and his inheritance for a neighboring nation that was a mortal enemy of his own people. In Moab, he would be challenged to remain openly a Jew, to not hide his real identity. His challenge would be to just fit in and worship whatever gods were presented to him. This would be a real challenge since he just came out from under the leadership of the God of his fathers'. At this point, he'd feel very little connection to *YHWH* in Moab.

No, Elimelech entered the land of compromise. And many of us have walked the same road he did. Unfortunately, we know this road all too well.

We see that in time Elimelech died in the land of compromise. It reminds me of the wisdom of Solomon. I often wonder if Solomon was thinking of his great-great-grandfather Elimelech when he penned these words: "There is a way that seems right to a man, but its end is the way of death" (Prov. 14:12). (Boaz would have been the literal great-great grandfather of Solomon. However, Boaz was fulfilling the rights of a kinsman-redeemer, making Elimelech also an ancestor of Solomon.)

As we close out this chapter, I'm challenged afresh with understanding the times in which I live. I'm challenged in my understanding that there is a mighty difference between the love of God for an individual and His judgments for a generation.

Our tension is that of Elimelech's. Our generation's identity, imbedded deeply in our hearts, is to see King Jesus return to the earth and rule from Jerusalem. The contradiction and tension is found in that we know this inside of our hearts, but are we properly discerning the events that will usher in His heavenly Kingdom? We're not seeing that the return of Jesus comes in the context of the temporal judgments of God against wickedness (Rev. 6, 8–9, 16). And we're not seeing our role in these events as important to the souls of humanity around us as they slip into eternity every day.

We cannot and must not try to manage these tensions divorced from corporate night-and-day fasting and prayer. God has no contradiction with the corporate national reality of wickedness that fans the flames of His zeal against us. He is forever righteous and true altogether.

No, unsanctified mercy tells us everything will be fine.

Unsanctified mercy allows us to believe lies, hide our heads in the proverbial sand and carry on, perpetuating our ungodly dreams that blind us to the dreams of God's heart.

If we truly love Him, will we surrender our dreams for His? Are we living our lives well if we seek to do only that which matched the cry and desire of His heart? And would that be enough for you and me?

With this in mind, our only appeal to Him that will have any impact is an appeal for mercy with a heart torn open to the truth (Joel 2:12–17)!

Shall we get started? Shall we learn how to partner with Him in mercy?

CHAPTER 10

Partners of Mercy

*"'You shall make a mercy seat of pure gold.... And
you shall make two cherubim of gold; of hammered
work you shall make them...'" (Exod. 25:17–18).*

Jesus and Father are looking for friends, looking for partners who embrace the boundaries given to them and disallow unsanctified mercy to have its way. The Godhead is looking for partners of true mercy.

Father God has always wanted a Bride for His Son who was altogether like Him, created in His image and likeness. Such a Bride will walk with Him, turn to Him and live for Him, even in the midst of difficulty and dark painful circumstances. That's who Father is seeking.

True love by its definition is voluntary, offered freely from the will at any and all times. Love is easy to offer in good times, but loving someone when life gets hard is a different matter. One of the greatest vows made by married couples is to remain faithful to one another "for better, for worse." I'm blessed with a wife who holds to that vow when I give her every reason to shut down and walk away. She evidences God's goodness and mercy to me.

And God's mercy has brought restoration to us all, to all our wounded hearts when we needed Him most! It's just the way He is; He can't be any other way.

We read many stories that demonstrate this truth, but I want to draw your attention to two of them. One is the building of the ark of the covenant, and the other is Abraham's offering Isaac on the altar.

Let's look at Abraham's story first.

We are very familiar with this story. Abraham and Sarah were together for years, and she was unable to conceive. God promised them an heir. Abraham believed God, and it was credited to his account in heaven as faith.

After about twenty years, God made good on the promise, and Sarah had Isaac. In time, God called Abraham to do something very unorthodox. He was commanded by God to take Isaac to Mount Moriah and sacrifice him on the altar Abraham was to build. Abraham followed through and got to the place where his son was on the altar. His hand gripped the knife raised over Isaac's heart. God saw that Abraham was willing to do what he was commanded to do. God said to him, "Because you have done this thing, and have not withheld your son, your only son—blessing I will bless you, and multiplying I will multiply your descendants..." (Gen. 22:16–17).

You see, God was looking for someone to join Him in partnership and friendship. It was as if He were asking, "Can I ask Abraham to do something unorthodox like carrying a burden that I carry? Can I ask Abraham to do the impossible just for the sake of being a prophetic picture of something that I will really do? Will he get mad at Me when I call him not only to faith in Me but also into friendship with Me, into true partnership? Will he stay with Me when it gets tough? When pressures emerge and there seems to be no escape, will he be My friend and share in the emotional burden of what only I can really do? Only I can sacrifice My Son and have it count for all time."

Abraham's obedient act displayed a prophetic picture

to humanity of what God would do to deal with the deadly condition of sin in the hearts of men and women. He found in Abraham someone to bear the burden with Him, someone who would not be offended by His request. And God, the greater Abraham, had no one to stay His own hand (Isa. 53:10).

Do you hear what I'm saying? Only God could take the life of His Son and have it count for all time. God was looking for a faith and mercy partner. And Abraham became it! He learned faith and mercy. He was challenged to believe that God had a plan for his son's salvation and return. He held the knife poised over not just his son's heart, but his own heart too, and he stood there at the mercy of God. And he still obeyed, evidencing his willingness to partner with God in whatever it was He was looking to do.

James 2 tells us God called Abraham, the one who offered up his son at His request, *friend*. It's like I can hear in my mind God say, "Abraham, now you are My friend. You know how this feels and how this moves My heart. Abraham, hold your knife, stay your hand, lay not your hand on the boy. Abraham, let Me be merciful to you right now. Stop! But Abraham, what will bring you mercy forever will cost Me everything! Mercy to you, Abraham, costs Me much! You got it! Thank you for hearing Me out and letting Me show you this."

Abraham's faith was strengthened into friendship. God's relationship with Abraham started with simple obedience but developed over years into a friendship that went way beyond the "what you can do for me" kind of faith. God formed an everlasting friendship with Abraham. Like clay in the potter's hand, Abraham was at the mercy of God, and he allowed the hand of God to form his heart.

Hold that thought for a moment. Let's look next at the construction of the ark of the covenant.

Exodus 25 gives us the blueprints and instructions for

the building of this most precious furnishing of the tabernacle of Moses. This piece was to be the very residence of God on the earth inside of the tabernacle system. It was built in a very specific way and for a particular purpose.

Once built, it would be sprinkled with blood once a year to cover the sin of the people. It was to contain the Ten Commandments, the rod of Aaron and some of the manna given by God to feed His people. But what attracts my attention was the lid of the ark called the *mercy seat.*

Made of solid gold, the mercy seat was where the sacrificial blood was applied. Also on this lid were placed two cherubim facing one another with their wings covering over the seat. While the lid was made of pure gold, these cherubim were also solid but not cast. Here's where this plan touches me. These cherubim were hammered, not cast, into their shape. They were attached to the mercy seat by God's design after being hammered into place.

What an object lesson this should be for us. (Work with me on this one.) Abraham was willing to find friendship with God at the mercy seat through the hammering process that formed and fashioned his faith. Every step, every choice, every obedient act of his helped shape him into God's friend. There are times where God is forming mercy in us, and His work of friendship comes from our being hammered by Him. As we allow Him to work this process in our lives, as we say *yes* to His hammering, we become merciful. We must have the same content of material in us that the mercy seat is made of.

God promised, "And there [between the outstretched hammered wings of the angels and his solid gold lid called the *mercy seat*] *I will meet with you, and I will speak with you from above the mercy seat and from between the cherubim...*" (Exod. 25:22, emphasis added). At His mercy seat, He will speak to you. At His mercy seat, He will shape you and cover you with His love [blood]. At His mercy seat, He will receive your humble pleas for friendship as you share with Him the burdens of His heart.

With a hammer in His hand, He takes the gold substance of your life, softens it in the fire, taps it into place and calls it *His mercy seat*. You become His friend. Your relationship goes way beyond what He can do for you and enters into a place where angels fear to tread!

The mercy seat, overshadowed by hammered golden angels, is a hallowed place. Don't be so quick to jump or run from the fiery trials that hammer your shape into a form that overshadows the mercy seat. The Lord is working endurance and perseverance into you. He is fashioning a friend, and so few choose to go there.

To which of the angels has He given friendship. His angels are His ministering spirits sent to serve His purposes in the lives of men. But which of the angels did He call friend? Which of them did He invite into His deepest councils regarding bearing the emotional content of His heart?

No, it is to us and us alone that He offers friendship. It starts with obedience to His unorthodox ways and means.

It is my belief that faith is strengthened in so many different places and in various means. But it is my solemn conviction that you find friendship with God as you are hammered into place at His mercy seat. And there you find the blessing of His mercy.

CHAPTER 11

Mercy's Blessed

"'Blessed are the merciful, for they shall obtain mercy'"
(Matt. 5:7).

Not long into my son Jordan's seventh-grade year, he began to confront some deep heart issues from past relationships. Father God had touched him early in life, and he
was learning the principle of mercy and forgiveness in the
face of injustice.

While our family was on the mission field in Eastern Eu-
rope, Jordan had been beaten often on the playground by the
bullies of the block. It was a rough time, and no matter how
many times he would try to reconcile and resolve the confron-
tations, nothing worked. He spent many lonely hours searching for good friends, but there were too few.

After returning home to Canada from Poland, he faced
the same issues. Our first year home, Jordan was in sixth
grade. That was one rough year; it was an incredibly lonely
one. I thought we got all our heart issues worked out by the
end of sixth grade, but not long into seventh grade, in a new
school with new opportunities, I noticed a very strange thing
happening: Jordan was sabotaging his friendships! Instead of
his peers initiating the conflicts, he appeared to be the one

picking the fights and seemingly with little or no reason whatsoever!

One night, as I sat on his bed talking with him about life, the whole thing opened up. I think it was Holy Spirit wanting to help. You know, you can only carry hurt, anger, bitterness and unforgiveness for so long before they spill out on those around you.

In times past, Jordan had not evidenced bitterness in his life. And so it was very noticeable when it surfaced. Though my heart hurt for him, I knew it was time to slay that serpent.

As we talked that night, the deep hurt and anger in his heart became apparent, and they obviously had led him to make some destructive decisions. He began telling me things under the influence of his woundedness. He said, "Dad, no one wants to be my friend! And friends always hurt you or beat you. I might as well get them first before they get me! I don't know why they think I'm not a good friend."

Jordan went from one lie, to a partial truth, to revenge and finally to a self-depreciating statement. I knew he was in a dangerous place, and I started getting angry myself. I could feel that evil snake wrapping its coils around my son, and there was no way this was going any further. We had always taught our kids the principle of forgiveness and mercy. However, I was being challenged because my understanding of justice was so poor.

I saw three things that needed to happen. Jordan needed to forgive, he needed to be empowered to stand his ground securely while under attack, and I needed to learn about justice.

As we activated the principles of forgiveness and mercy that night, I watched weights of oppression lift from my son's soul. The light returned to his eyes. He forgave as face after face of angry offenders came before mind's recollection. Each one he forgave, and each time I saw oppression leave him.

As we finished, we asked the Lord to give Jordan true friends, ones who were good and faithful. We prayed and asked the Lord to show him where his friends were.

The next day Jordan came home absolutely excited. (We say *jacked up* in Missouri.) He was waiving this permission slip from one of the coaches at school. My jaw dropped to the floor when I saw that it was for the wrestling team! You have to understand that Jordan weighed maybe 100 pounds at the time, *maybe*! He was a skinny rack of bones and sinew. Though I somehow couldn't see him at his size become a wrestler on the team, his passion soon won me over. I recognized that God was doing something in it.

I wasn't sure what was going to happen. I half expected this rush of testosterone to flame out with his first loss. I was planning for failure. I needed to repent! But I was getting way ahead of myself. I just signed the paper and prayed, "Father, I hope You know what You're doing!"

Three weeks later, I went to Jordan's first wrestling meet. The guys in his age bracket were huge, and I was sure some of them had failed a few grades!

As he faced his first giant, I was touched by the brightness in his eyes. The guy was way bigger than he, but Jordan really thought he could take him.

As Jordan stepped onto the mat with his first opponent, I tried to coach him. Most of my fear-based stammering words amounted to run away and wait for the right moment. Jordan just looked at me with a frown, reassuring me that wasn't his plan.

Jordan and this kid who looked like Hulk Hogan's son, faced each other and prepared for war. The referee lowered his upraised arm and blew his whistle to start the match

The overconfident adversary made the first move, lunging at him. I'm proud to say that was the giant's last! My son sidestepped, pivoted, grabbed the guy's mid-section, used his momentum against him and threw him down. Stunned, the

large group huddled around the wrestling mat, let out this corporate *whoa* as Jordan pinned the kid in about fifteen seconds!

The opponent slumped off the mat as people around me
said, "Who's that kid? Where's he from?"

Turning to them, I smiled and said, "That's my boy!"

Jordan didn't win because he had the most weight or
greatest strength. He won because of his technique. In the
weeks that followed, he consistently pinned guys bigger and
stronger than he as he used their raw strength against them.

It was a joy to watch him. I would sit next to parents
from the opposing school before each bout and listen to their
commentary about how they expected my kid to be pinned
in record time. I loved the shocked look on their faces when
my skinny kid would pin their kid to the mat! It was the gap-
ing jaw and deep furrowed frown of confusion on their faces
that did it for me!

Another reason I went to watch Jordan wrestle was for
the expression on his face each time he won. The referee
would hold his hand high as they stood in the middle of the
mat in front of everyone. My son would smile that smile of
victory and satisfaction. I will always remember the expression on his face. When they put the medal around his neck as
the tournament winner in his grade bracket, all I could think
was how thankful I was that my son was no longer under the
venomous oppression of bitterness.

Yes, Jordan did have some defeats, but in those shock-
ing victories something had happened to him. He was learning to stand his ground, face larger obstacles and still expect
to win. He was learning to win graciously and lose without
shame and humiliation.

Jordan developed friendships that were healthy, team-
oriented and empowering. He always wanted to practice his
moves on me, and I loved it. He was coming alive. His confidence was returning.

I believe that something broke open for Jordan the night

he forgave his enemies. The night he was merciful, I believe mercy was released to him.

He had new healthy friendships—mercy for his past loneliness. He was being empowered to stand his ground securely under attack—mercy for his past lack of confidence.

Then came the moment of truth.

Healed from the old wounds and scars, Jordan treated one of his friends in an unkind way. It was totally out of character and uncalled for. His friend was in the same place he had been just a few weeks earlier. When it was pointed out to him, Jordan's heart was crushed. He felt so bad and ashamed.

"Dad, what do I do?" he asked, his head down and eyes wet with tears.

I showed him Matthew 5:7, "'Blessed are the merciful, for they shall obtain mercy.'"

He was facing a very humbling but important moment. He had known the sting of being offended, but the reality of being the offender was humbling him further.

The next day at school he apologized to his friend and asked for forgiveness. He was standing his ground on the principles of the Scriptures, humbly asking for mercy.

That night at bedtime, I sat again on his bed, listening to his version of the story. He was relieved that his friend had forgiven, had shown mercy. It was a powerful revelation for him. And, I must add, a defining moment in his life. He had passed a huge test. He had wrestled a very important opponent called *pride*; he had stood his ground while under attack and had done the right thing.

He realized that in his life, it is better to be merciful and forgiving for there would always be moments where he would need mercy himself.

Can you hear the whisper of the Spirit in this? He's saying, "Blessed are the merciful, blessed are those who are full of mercy, for they shall obtain mercy."

CHAPTER 12

Full of Mercy

"The wisdom that is from above is...full of mercy..."
(James 3:17).

When Scripture uses the word *full* or *fullness,* it's talking about a place where we are consistently walking in the fullness of a particular attribute of God. Take, for example, Stephen. Acts 9:8–10 says he was "full of faith and power." What does that mean?

It means that Stephen's heart was emptied of his own wisdom and striving for power. His being full also spoke of perfection or maturity.

In Luke 4, we are told that Jesus came from His baptism in the Jordan "filled with the Holy Spirit," and that after His temptation in the wilderness He returned in the "power of the Spirit." He went to the wilderness *full of the Spirit* and returned *full of power in the Spirit.* What had happened to Him? He had been transformed through testing and trial.

We are told about Dorcas in Acts 9:36. She was "full of good works and charitable deeds."

Stephen, Jesus and Dorcas are examples of people who had a significant work of God done in their hearts. Testing, trials, pressures, all coupled with temptations that come from the world, the flesh and the devil—these play an important part in God's grand plan to *fill* each one of us with Himself.

Ephesians 4:11–12 tells us that the Church has been gifted by Jesus with ministry giftings (apostles, prophets, evangelists, pastors and teachers) for the equipping of the saints for works of service. These gifts are given to us "for the edifying of the body of Christ, till we all come to the unity of the faith and *of the knowledge of the Son of God, to a perfect man, to the measure of the stature of the fullness of Christ*" (v. 13, emphasis added).

The purpose of these ministry gifts is to lead, teach and train us in greater depths of fullness in Christ. The goal of Father is a Church that has been purified and made spotless, looking more and more like the Head, Jesus.

Now, having said all that, I have a few questions. What are the pressures the Lord will place on us that will call forth a wisdom that is full of mercy? How do we get to a place where our desires for carnal justice are surpassed by the power of godly mercy?

I must freely confess that I have no idea. I do know that Jesus desires to give us mercy. We have talked about this, but let's take one step farther. He is full of mercy and considers mercy great wisdom. We all don't always have the fullness of mercy working in us. Fortunately, this will change one day; in fact, it's changing even now.

I believe before this life is done, He will find a way to call forth many in mercy. I'm trembling about it because I know that my self-centered, self-loving, American self will find this somewhat offensive.

What would it be like to step beyond our basic self-centered, narcissistic, religious focus into a new realm of the knowledge of God? What if we decide to take God at His Word and enter into a new place of wisdom that is full of mercy and good fruit? What if we believe that there is mercy for those who ask, cleansing for those who seek and faith for those who doubt? What would happen if we actually believed?

I think our lives would be similar to those portrayed in the movie, *Braveheart*. It's a stunning, though bloody, historical fiction about William Wallace and his fight to free Scotland from English tyranny and rule.

The Scottish King, William the Bruce, in a discussion with his conniving father, described the way Wallace fought. He said Wallace fought with passion and that his men followed and loved him.

His father moved on to discuss titles, properties and lands when the young Bruce interjected, "I don't want more titles and lands. I want to fight. I want to believe!"

The Bruce, as they called him, recognized something in Wallace that he did not have. He saw Wallace had faith for a higher value than himself.

Wallace valued freedom with a higher regard than his own life and the collection of titles and lands—yes, even beyond the comforts of his own life.

So what does this have to do with being full of mercy and good fruit? What does this have to do with wisdom that is full of mercy?

It's the evidence of men and women who have been emptied of their own comforts and seen the call to a higher, wider, longer, deeper value—the value of living beyond their self-promoting ways and bitter envies, the value of placing others ahead of their own comforts and needs, the value of placing mercy ahead of the easy way, the broad way.

Sometimes fullness in mercy means work and sacrifice for you and me. It means it might look like the other guy has won while we have lost though we know in God's eyes this is not the case.

What if we sought for the other guy to win in God before we ever considered ourselves? What if we looked beyond ourselves and sought for fullness in others first? What would

that look like? Would that be the actual picture of being full
of mercy?

I believe the picture of being full of mercy is like the picture Jesus described when He spoke of the fields being white
unto harvest (John 4:35). I can see us being full of mercy and
it resulting in a great harvest of souls.

CHAPTER 13

Mercy's Harvest

"'The harvest is truly plentiful, but the laborers few'"
(Matt. 9:37).

We are living in one of the greatest hours of human history. And we are about to witness an unprecedented outpouring of Holy Spirit that will far surpass even the mighty revival of Jerusalem on the Day of Pentecost.

This coming revival will be the fullness of what Peter preached would come in the last days as prophesied by Joel. This revival will be global in scope, stunning in its signs and wonders, heart-melting to the wicked, cataclysmic to the supernatural powers of darkness, glorious to the redeemed and *merciful* to those who respond to the call of the gospel!

There is just one problem: We really need more laborers! Jesus looked out on a world that was harassed and lost, wandering its way through life, and said, "The harvest truly is plentiful, but the laborers are few" (Matt. 9:37). The problem He saw wasn't a lack of work. There was and is plenty of work to do; He told us so. The issue was and is the number of the labor force.

In a way, the ability to gather in the harvest is greatly affected by the number of workers who participate in it. Having only a few workers affects the fullness of the harvest. I married into a family that has deep roots in the farming community. Both my mother- and father-in-law come from farming families in the Canadian Breadbasket of Saskatchewan.

Harvest time in the mid 1900s meant long hours of hard work with every available worker gathering the harvest into the barns. Often meals were brought to the fields, and whole extended families would travel from field to field, helping one another gather their crops.

The harvesting was done with teams of horses driving the threshing machinery that looked ancient compared to today's high-powered combines. There was a joy in the work for the waiting was over, and the time had come to reap the rewards of their hard labor and months of waiting, watching, praying for rain and waiting some more. At times their work involved not merely preparing the fields, but they spent hours repairing the equipment used for harvest.

Consider the faith of a farmer who bought tools for the harvest. He planned for a day he hoped would come. He was so dependent on the weather, the seasonal conditions and the absence of pests that could destroy his hard work.

Life as a harvester is truly a walk of faith. Yet Jesus told us in Matthew 9:37 that the greatest issue regarding the harvest at the end of the age wouldn't be the harvesting tools or the pesky pests or devilish demons who come to steal the harvest. It wouldn't be the weather conditions either. "Will we have laborers?" That was the observation He made and the question He implied.

Furthermore, Jesus was concerned about it enough to make it a prayer point for His followers and fellow workers. He said, "Pray the Lord of the harvest to send out laborers" (Matt. 9:38).

The bottom line is the harvest requires more workers, more laborers. If you want a job in the end-time harvest, you've got one. If you want to be one of the harvesters of human souls during the closing hours of human history, you'll be one. Presently there are preparations to be done, tools to be bought, repairs to be made in order to ready yourself for this next outpouring.

I believe we have at least two great waves of harvest coming—one very, very soon and the other in the closing hours during the Great Tribulation. There may be more, but I clearly see these two coming.

The closest wave I believe is like unto the story in Matthew 20 of the landowner who called workers into his fields all throughout the day in order to get the work done. This wave will be what I might call the *harvest of the harvesters!*

This will be the harvest of those laborers meant to participate in Jesus' end-time harvest field. He will bring them out of darkness into light that they might be workers during a very joyful time in His Kingdom.

Many, who I believe will be in the first wave, are currently chained to bar stools, drowning in alcohol. Others are tied to bedposts, prostituting themselves or being held against their will with no hope of escape. They're piercing their skin with needles or drawing up their lines of cocaine ready to draw on their straw. At this moment, they're bowing before financial idols.

The Lord of the harvest is looking for laborers right now. He's looking to harvest them before He begins the end-time harvest.

Perhaps you've counted yourself out due to your behaviors or brokenness. Let me assure you that He's first harvesting His harvesters. He's coming after those who started out meaning well but have quickly slipped into lives that hold them bound in chains like a prisoner.

In His mercy, Jesus is preparing those who will accept His offer of mercy, step away from the bonds, whatever they may be, and begin afresh with their lives in God.

This first harvest is to invite you to participate in the

preparations for the final end-time harvest of souls. The very one that will occur before Christ's return to the earth. You're being called to prepare, no matter how long it takes, for His work of harvesting souls.

This means hours of preparation with the tools of the harvest—hours in prayer, fasting and serving faithfully where He shows you how to work. This means days and years of searching His Word for His heart for the future and for sharpening your sickle. It means preparing *His* way for it's *His* harvest.

His preparation plan is simple and inexpensive to the natural eye. It may mean changing friends, jobs, homes or even city locations. It may mean you lose everything this present age has to offer, but in the end it will be worth it.

This is Mercy's Harvest. This is the gathering of those who have walked the roads of indulgence, having at one time known the truth. This is the gathering of men and women who think it's too late for them but want the grace to believe a greater truth. It's the ingathering of those who want to *get over* themselves and *get on* with God.

Recently the Lord was helping me to *get over* something. A real depression hit me one day, opening up a pocket of resistance within me. God was cleansing my heart regarding my motivations and ultimately getting to some heart issues with my identity. I was fighting it but was losing the battle, and I was angry about it. My issue was envy.

I had been prayer reading through Psalm 73, focusing on Asaph's response to the lack of justice regarding the lifestyles of the wicked. He was asking the question, "Why God?"

I was in that same place. My bank account was low, and I had no plan on what to do. I was just feeling the weight of my material situation. I had left a well paying job in Canada to move to IHOP-KC and was feeling the challenges of that move. The pain of paying a mortgage when I had helped so many pay off their houses was getting to me. God was pushing on something in my heart using all the triggers he could to surface the pain and envy. "For I was envious of the boastful, when I saw the prosperity of the wicked," Asaph said (Ps. 73:3). "My feet had almost stumbled, my steps had nearly slipped" (v. 2).

I was also triggered by condemnation. Demonic accusation had seized the open door and had begun weighing my mind down with lies. "You wasted so much time in the past. You should be farther along in life, more well known, but no you blew it. You wasted years you will never get back."

The pressure was increasing. I needed the love of God to break the silence, tear down the lies and speak truth. I was asking the Lord for help and getting ready to do my part to help at our national conference when the answer came.

I was looking forward to hearing the guest speaker at the conference hosted by IHOP-KC. I was wrestling with envy and saw a friend of mine ministering prophetically to a *celebrity* couple on the front row. My heart was so wrong, and I knew it. I grew more upset. As I think about it now, I realize it was awesome because God had me in a headlock and wasn't letting me go.

Just that morning in my prayer time, I asked the Lord to help me quickly deal with envy and not let it grow. I asked Holy Spirit to speak to me then and there. I prayed that He would break the atmosphere of anger if I ever let it get that far. Later that day I was in what I can only call an *envy seizure*. Right in the middle of my envious thoughts, watching my friend minister, Holy Spirit broke in with such a clear voice. He asked me, "How many people are in this conference room right now?"

Though I'm not good with numbers, our room was full because of the guest speaker there. We had chairs to the front of the platform, chairs on the back walls—it was packed!

"Oh, I don't know," I said. I really didn't know, but I responded anyway, "I'll say about 2,000!"

Quickly, the Lord shot back, "How many is your friend praying for?"

I could count that number without any difficulty. "Three!" I said. And the answer hit me.

"Well then, that leaves 1,997 for you. Why don't you get busy?"

Suddenly the weight of His answer hit me, and Matthew 9:37–38 washed over me, "...the harvest is plentiful, but the *laborers are few*" (emphasis added). I felt so totally overwhelmed at the number in front of me. If I wanted a job, I had one. Otherwise, I could just continue to sit there angry and envious.

I wanted my pay right there. I wanted to enjoy the rewards of praying for the celebrity couple. It kept me from seeing the rest of the room, from seeing those who were equally important to God.

I turned around and laid hands on the man behind me. The words the Lord gave me ministered to his heart. I moved across the aisle and laid hands on another, and the power of God hit that person. I stepped up to another, and in their words, "It was like chains fell off me when you touched me."

I was so locked up in my envy and sinful attitude, disqualifying myself as to why I couldn't help, all the while missing the very work right in front of me. Someone has to be His hands extended. Someone has to be His voice spoken out with grace and truth. Someone has to be the ax that hits the roots, delivering a heart from bondage.

And that's why I can say this to you: If you want a job in the harvest, you've got one! There is a preparation plan and pre-harvest work to be done, but if you're willing to do that work, He has a job for you. It may not be with celebrities, but trust me, it will be meaningful to Him. And, in the end, isn't that all that matters? Let's participate in the harvest. Let's show forth His mercy and His goodness to the ends of the earth, persevering and enduring until He comes!

CHAPTER 14

Enduring Mercy

"'O Israel, you will not be forgotten by Me!'" (Isa. 44:21).

*I*n a previous chapter, I shared some precious memories of Beth, our daughter. One such moment came in her fourteenth year with us. She had been reading Ezekiel and found a very profound passage in the first fourteen verses of chapter 16.

In this section God prophesied regarding Jerusalem. Ezekiel told Jerusalem about her history and then asked a critical question. God wanted to know why Jerusalem had turned away from Him when He had taken her from a place of abandonment and made her a great princess. Verses 4–5 read as follows:

> *"On the day you were born your navel cord was not cut, nor were you washed in water to cleanse you; you were not rubbed with salt nor wrapped in swaddling cloths. No eye pitied you, to do any of these things for you, to have compassion on you; but you were thrown out into the open field, when you yourself were loathed on the day you were born."*

God reminded Jerusalem that she was like an abandoned

child who had not been pitied and cared for on the day of her birth. She wasn't washed; she wasn't cleansed. But when God found her, He took pity on her and took her in. The next verses read, "'And when I passed by you and saw you struggling in your own blood, I said to you in your blood, "Live!" Yes, I said to you in your blood, "Live!" I made you thrive like a plant in the field; and you grew, matured, and became very beautiful'" (vv. 6–7).

God saw her condition—abandoned and left to struggle alone—He washed her, dressed her, set her in a place of honor and caused her to thrive.

This had been the story of our Beth. When Cheryl found her at eleven days old, she still hadn't been cleaned from her birth. She was sick, crying out for food and struggling for life. The nurse tried to convince Cheryl not to take *that baby*.

"She will be stupid just like her birth mother! I sent that girl three times for an abortion, and she couldn't do it!" was the nurse's hurtful statement.

Cheryl finished the process of adoption and brought Beth home to me, and we've loved her ever since. We've clothed her, loved her and cared for her when she was sick—you know, she's ours!

But on this one day in Beth's fourteenth year, she came to me having read through Ezekiel 16. And in her matter of fact way, she asked me, "Have you ever read Ezekiel 16, daddy? Do you know what's in it?"

After a brief exchange over the content, Beth said something that crushed my heart. I just bawled when she walked away. She said, "Daddy, thank you! Ezekiel 16:1–14 is *my* story! You found me, washed me, clothed me, fed me and treated me like a princess! Thank you, daddy! This is love. This is *God's love*. This is the same love that God has in His heart for Jerusalem!"

Talk about understanding, she got the truths expressed in Ezekiel 16. It caused her to volunteer unsolicited thankfulness for the life she had been given. Such gratitude is a powerful weapon for sustaining the human heart in God. What an incredible moment!

There were several reasons my heart was touched that day. It wasn't only Beth's gratitude that so affected me. But I was awestruck by the continuing way the Lord speaks to me. Even today, I'm amazed at how He teaches me through the intricacies of my daughter's adoption.

Another thing touched me from Beth's comment, and it was Father God's deep tenderness for Jerusalem and Israel. You see, the literal context of Ezekiel 16 is a prophecy to Jerusalem and eventually to Israel as a whole. We must see it as such first and foremost. Before we use this text in any other way, we must see this chapter in its context.

I was left broken in a positive way that day. Since then, Holy Spirit has begun to speak to me about other things on His heart.

For example, on a later date, He said, "Dale, the Father still feels this way for Israel and Jerusalem." I could feel the emotion of the moment, and my heart was opened to the impartation of God that came with Holy Spirit's words.

If we're going to talk about mercy, then *we must* talk about God's heart for wandering Israel and Jerusalem. Though He has done all that Ezekiel speaks of, the nation has not walked in the revelation, the gratitude and thankfulness of her royalty. There is a present remnant, however, who are grateful, and we thank God for them.

For the most part, though, Israel and her capital Jerusalem are no different than the Gentile nations around her. Called to walk as a royal princess, she treads the streets as any common harlot.

Our problem comes when we look at her without the eyes of wisdom and revelation. When we don't know the heart of God, we have a common tendency to write off the ungrateful and unrepentant.

There are many around the world, churched or un-churched, who are filled with hatred for Israel. Some even accuse the Jews of having killed Jesus, and so they hate them. Others have their own reasons for despising Israel and her people.

As I've investigated the numerous reasons Israel is hated, I've found one main thought that causes so much upheaval and might be the root of it all.

God has chosen Israel to be servant leaders on the earth and has appointed His choice of King to lead the earth. Israel will be servant leaders alongside her Servant Ruler, Jesus, and will rule from the chosen capital of Jerusalem.

Not even all Israel believes this! So if a house is divided, how can it stand?

Whether or not we believe these facts to be true, they are in God's heart nonetheless. There is so much biblical evidence to support it, and most of it is being ignored by Gentile believers and the world in general.

Let's be clear. God has not changed His heart regarding Israel and Jerusalem. However, God is going to do a work of purification with Israel and all those who stand with her. He is going to remove the harlotry from her and cleanse her again as He did when He found her kicking and screaming in her own blood, abandoned among the nations of the earth.

God is faithful and will perform all that He has promised to Israel—not because of her faithfulness but because of His. He can be trusted to do all that He has promised.

In Isaiah 44:21, God tells Israel that she "will not be forgotten" by Him. And in Jeremiah 29:10, He tells Judah that she will be visited after seventy years in captivity and be set free to return to Israel and to Jerusalem, the city, so as to reestablish and rebuild it.

If we are going to talk about the mercy of God, if we are going to talk about a God who is rich in mercy, then we must talk about and receive His heart of mercy for Israel. He has shown mercy to you and me time and time again in a personal individual way; He will show that same mercy to nations if they ask for it. And we see in Scripture that Israel and her leaders will ask for it; they *will ask* for mercy.

Isaiah 28 tells us that Israel and her leaders will even make a covenant with death, a peace treaty with a dominant world leader who in the end will not spare them. Israel will think the leader will be merciful, but he'll turn on her and break the covenant in the end. We only know him as the anti-Christ, but one thing is for certain—he'll turn the table on her.

Two chapters later, in Isaiah 30, God tells us that He'll wait to be gracious to Israel. He'll wait until all her wisdom backs her into a corner of death with her only way out being an appeal to God for mercy. That's when He'll give it.

Why? Because God loves Israel. He took her from humble beginnings and made her royalty. Though she has walked away from Him, He will restore her in purity and humility.

Why? Because God loves, no, He *delights* in showing mercy. And he is determined that mercy will win.

I've heard many teach that God is done with Israel and that's why Jerusalem stands divided at this point in history. I can't agree to this. I believe that's unbiblical. In fact, I believe it violates the nature and character of God. He *is* merciful and will show mercy to Israel.

For us to believe this in our hearts, we must have revelation from God. Only He can put into us the desires and emotions He feels for Israel and Jerusalem.

The writer of Psalm 89 opened his song with a declaration of God's faithfulness and mercy to all generations. He sang, "I will sing of the mercies of the Lord forever; with my mouth will I make known Your faithfulness to all generations. For I have said, 'Mercy shall be built up forever; Your faithfulness You shall establish in the very heavens'" (v. 1).

No, we must open up our hearts to God's lasting

faithfulness, love and mercy for Israel. There are some good reasons for this.

I believe that the Scriptures teach us believers will be here on the earth during the Great Tribulation (Joel 1–2; Matt. 24; 1 Thess. 4:13–18; 5:1–10; 2 Thess. 2; 1 Tim. 4:1–2). Many debate and argue over these matters, but as I see it, Jew and Gentile will pass through (Isa. 43:1–3) a very terrible time of testing. It will be our greatest hour no matter how difficult it gets (Joel 2).

Many believe this tribulation is only for Israel as a punishment for her sins and for crucifying Jesus (Matt. 27:25). Many teach that she must face this on her own with no help at all from God or others (Ps. 20:2; 22:19; 40:17; Isa. 41:10–14; Mark 9:22). I believe such teaching to be inconsistent with the foundations of the Scriptures (Rom. 3:23; 6:23).

We need to know God's plan for Israel in these last days since He will use many Gentile believers as messengers to remind Israel of who she is (Isa. 40:1–5; Mal. 3:1; Rom. 10:14–15). These messengers will be part of God's end-time strategy. They will speak His love to her through their words and works.

God will not leave Israel alone (Zech. 14:1–5; John 14:18). She will have a true witness (Rev. 11:3), and this witness will proclaim the truth of God's heart to her. This proclamation will come with power to turn her heart because it will be full of the love (Jer. 31:3; Hosea 2:19; Rom. 5:5; 8:39; 1 Cor. 2:9; Eph. 5:25–32) and mercy of God towards her. It will be a message of truth, its content oozing with mercy.

And all Israel will be saved (Rom. 11:26)!

I am preparing myself for the day that God, in His mercy, will send messengers of righteousness to Israel, both Jew and Gentile. These will proclaim God's heart of compassion for the nation. I believe He'll raise up messengers in the nation and bring others from afar to boldly proclaim His love for her again. I believe there will be a remnant fully devoted to Him in the land before He returns. It's His promise and covenant to her—and He never breaks His promises.

I believe that the fact that Israel as a nation must deal with the tourism of Christian pilgrims to the Holy Land is a prophetic signpost to them. Every faithful Christian who tours Israel brings a message to the people whether they speak any words or not. It's telling them that God's eyes are still upon His people. He has not, nor will not, forsake them for His mercy endures forever toward them and us.

CHAPTER 15

The Government of Mercy

*"Let us therefore come boldly to the throne of grace,
that we may obtain mercy and find grace to
help in time of need" (Heb. 4:16).*

There is no mercy outside the Kingdom of God. No other
government, unless influenced by the Kingdom of Jesus, has the capability to demonstrate mercy.

Have you seen the recent movie released called *Fireproof*?
What a powerful movie! In the movie we saw individuals in
a marriage covenant who walked out from under the governmental leadership of God.

The husband, not walking with God but watching pornography and seeking his own way, found nothing but explosive rage manifesting toward his wife.

The wife, battered and beaten, not so much physically
as verbally and mentally, broke down and began looking for
understanding and tender arms to embrace her.

The void between them throughout the movie widened,
and we saw the obvious direction so many others in life have
taken. We saw the treachery of divorce beginning to emerge.

But then the man restored his relationship with God. He
surrendered anew to Jesus' governmental leadership of his

life. Though it took the cynical wife time to turn, in the end she did turn, and oh, what a turning it was!

I can imagine many today who seek to cast off the boundaries of a life lived for Jesus, saying the movie is just another piece of propaganda produced by the church, a group they consider to be a bigoted lot out of touch with reality. We must admit that the Church has propagated and continues to participate in sinful lusts. I say this to our shame but knowing it can change. In fact, I'm convinced it can change!

I say this not because of what I think people can do to reverse this terrible direction of our society but because of what I believe Jesus has in His heart for us and know what He's capable of doing. It's because of Him, because of who He is, that I have hope!

So what was it that turned around the marriage in *Fireproof*? As I mentioned before, the husband's decision to return to Christ was one thing that produced change. In his submitting himself to Christ's government, he was reestablishing his life under the leadership of Jesus the Merciful. He was returning to the Master of Mercy. The man learned the hard way that he couldn't step out from under Christ's leadership and still find mercy. It was and is impossible to find mercy anywhere apart from Christ. You will not get mercy from any governmental source save that which walks under the leadership of Jesus the Merciful!

As I said before, *doing* mercy is learned. When I see mercy resident within the life of a person, I become aware that either they or someone who influenced them actually knew Jesus or was somehow affected by Him.

Looking once again at the movie's storyline, the husband's decision to return to the Lord was tested. He had to then win back the heart of his wife. He had broken the relationship, so the burden was on him to do the work of restoring trust.

At first, his weak but sincere heart couldn't deal well

with his wife's rejection. She wasn't so easily won over. Her question was real—was his change sincere? Did he really love her?

The husband knew his change was sincere, and that meant he would have to demonstrate his sincerity by his actions. So he began to serve his wife's interests without expecting anything in return. Having received Christ's mercy in his innermost person, he began to walk under a different law—the law of love. Under Christ's governmental rule, the man would find peace in his relationship with his wife as he walked in love, as he continued to put his wife's interests and heart above his own.

Moved with the mercy that had been ministered to him at the cross, the husband took his savings meant for his own selfish purposes and bought much needed medical equipment for his mother-in-law. He did this with no fanfare, no warning to his wife or in-laws and no expectation of his wife returning to him at all. He did it because he saw a need, had the means to meet that need and did what he should. He was walking under a different governmental system, you see. He was exercising mercy and love in line with the government of Jesus the Merciful.

Without giving away the entire ending, at some point his mercy touched her. And when mercy touches a heart, it causes the heart to give itself away to the one who has extended it mercy.

Mercy offers us a clean slate, freedom from past failures and a new identity with which to stand before God. Mercy received grants strength to surrender our lives to love God and begin serving Him with love, abandon and gratitude for the rest of our days.

This is the government of God, the government of the Kingdom at work. Outside a living relationship with Him, mercy and abandoned love are impossible.

Other options are coming. Evil rulers and governmental

forces even now are planning their rise to power. They are making ready the laws by which they will govern and the punishment for those who will not receive their leadership. Please, I plead with you, there is only one Kingdom government of mercy. Only one! If you think there will be other, better options, you'll be disappointed.

Look at the systems of the earth as examples. There are men who motivate with fear, power, intrigue and threatening violence. Only Jesus has motivated the deep recesses of the human heart with love and mercy. As the King of the Kingdom of heaven, only He owns the keys that unlock the depths of the human heart. Only He knows how to impart the realities of His love and mercy into us. Only He can because He alone is merciful and He is love.

My prayer is for you to come into the government of Christ's mercy. I desire you to be so affected by His great love and mercy that you relinquish the reins of your heart to Him. It's time to dig the deepest well of gratitude you can by handing your life over to a new governmental system.

My prayer for those who are still cynical is that the next event of God's love will be the one that breaks your resistance to the sincerity of His love and mercy for you.

In the end, may we all find ourselves under the government of the Kingdom of God. May we find ourselves basking in the sunlight of the Man of Mercy, Jesus Christ. May we all find ourselves held in the power and grip of His mercy.

CHAPTER 16

The Cross of Mercy

"'Aaron shall lay both his hands on the head of the live goat, confess over it all the iniquities of the children of Israel, and all their transgressions, concerning all their sins, putting them on the head of the goat...'" (Lev. 16:21).

The cross of mercy is the cross of Jesus. It overshadows the Kingdom of mercy. And it's at the cross where we first find Him, Jesus, in all our disappointment, hurt, pain and sin.

The Son of God was the scapegoat for the sins of all mankind. Throughout the history of Israel, starting with Moses and his tabernacle in the wilderness, God has foreshadowed a plan so powerful that it was able to take the worst human atrocity, turn it around and make it the greatest manifestation of God's mercy.

In one moment of time, the focal point of all human history—the wrath of God, the rage of Satan and the curse of sin resting on men—was expressed. In one moment, God was able to declare His total hatred for the injustices of man's sin and express His undying love in removing the punishment for that sin to a scapegoat, to His Son.

As Aaron the high priest placed both his hands on the head of the scapegoat transferring all the sin of the camp to the sacrifice, so Father at the cross placed His hands on His Son, transferring all the sin and punishment of the camp to Him.

The cross of mercy washes me clean through the blood of Jesus. Pure and holy blood, innocent blood shed by murder covers the sin of murder.

What a magnificent mercy strategy. Think of it! The very blood of an innocent Man murdered on a cross removes from the repentant the very sin of murder! Unbelievable!

The cross of mercy is a wooden stake driven by Father to lay claim to the people of the earth. Like a pioneer staking his territory, like a gold miner filing his just claim, the cross is Father's survey marker that everything throughout the rest of human history must be measured by. His just claim trumps all others.

The cross is the ancient boundary stone that no one can nor dare move!

The cross of mercy enables me to step into Father's embrace. In essence, I come home to the identity first planned for me by Father's design. I come into the form and fashion of the dream of God's heart when He thought of me and knit me together in my mother's womb.

My body becomes the arena in which my love for the Trinity is worked out. My life becomes the love gift He has reserved for Himself on the earth. As I offer my love back to Him, His heart feels great delight.

The bloodstained cross is the only place where justice and mercy kiss! The deepest ugliest part of my dark humanity comes clean under the cascading crimson flow.

And finally, the cross is the place where I, on a consistent weekly basis, visit in confession of my weaknesses and inabilities to walk faithfully in this age. The cross deals with my broken humanity, twisted ways and hidden offenses that rust the inner core of my frame.

At the cross, I can speak freely, knowing that all is covered.

At the cross, I am named *Forgiven* not Forsaken and *Cherished* not Forgotten!

The cross draws a map in the sands of time, and calls me to anchor myself to the one place on earth that will never be shaken, even in the end-time judgments of God.

Golgotha leads me to a cross and then to a throne.

Rightly did Isaiah prophesy:

Now it shall come to pass in the latter days that the mountain of the LORD's house shall be established on the top of the mountains, and shall be exalted above the hills; and all nations shall flow to it. Many people shall come and say, "Come, and let us go up to the mountain of the LORD, to the house of the God of Jacob; He will teach us His ways, and we shall walk in His paths." For out of Zion shall go forth the law, and the word of the LORD from Jerusalem (Isa. 2:2–3).

Isaiah speaks of a time when the Lord's house will be established above all the hills of the earth and the nations will come to it in Jerusalem. All the earth will come and hear the teaching of Jesus on the mountain of His just claim. In Jerusalem, from Golgotha, Jesus the Lamb of God will teach us His ways, the way of the cross.

If any man would come to Him, he must deny himself, pick up his cross and follow Him (Luke 9:23–24). He is still the Servant of the Lord (Isa. 42:1–2) and will always be. When He comes, there will be no more cross to bear for His people, but it will still stand as an everlasting memorial to His love and tender compassion, to His great mercy.

And from the exact same spot, He will dispense His justice as the King of the earth seated on His throne.

To those who receive Him, His tender voice will shepherd and guide them into all truth. To those who refuse Him, the Lion's roar will be loud and His bite real.

In His mercy and desire to show love and justice, if He

doesn't bear the wrath of God for you on the cross, you will face the wrath of God alone at the judgment seat on that day.

There was only one Man able and willing and only one place built to bear the weight of all God could dish out that day.

Are you willing to bet eternity that you have a wiser mercy strategy than the cross of Christ? Are you sure you can present another man more loving, more merciful that will satisfy Father's judgment?

No, there's no other place. There's no other person.

In the face of Jesus, at the cross, you and I meet mercy personified. This is where we move from having learned about mercy into experiencing the true power of mercy. And only here are we empowered to "do justly, love mercy, and walk humbly" with our God (Mic. 6:8).

Order Form

	Qty.	Price	Total

MERCY WINS:

Learning Mercy in a Merciless Age _____ $ 10.00 _____

Subtotal _____

Shipping, Add 10 % (Minimum of $4.00) _____

Missouri Residents Add 7.725 % Sales Tax _____

Total Enclosed _____

U.S. Funds Only

Send payment with order to: Oasis House
PO Box 522
Grandview, MO 64030-0522

Name: _____

Address: Street _____

City _____ State _____

Zip _____

For quantity discounts and MasterCard/VISA or international orders, call 816-767-8880 or order on our fully secure website: www.oasishouse.net.

You can contact Dale at:
daleanderson@ihop.org
www.forallnations.wordpress.com